NEW YORK CITY

TRADITIONS

A view of Manhattan taken from the Staten Island Ferry

Viewing of a Renoir at the Metropolitan Museum of Art

Singer, Phil Ochs at a New York political rally, 19

NEW YORK CITY

TRADITIONS

Time Square by night

hamlyn

Publishing Director Laura Bamford
Executive Editor Mike Evans
Editors Jo Lethaby, Michelle Pickering
Production Controller Julie Hadingham
Picture Research Caroline Hensman

Creative Director Keith Martin
Design Geoff Borin

First published in 1998 by **Hamlyn**, an imprint of Reed Consumer
Books Limited, Michelin House, 81 Fulham Road, London SW3 6RB
and Auckland, Melbourne, Singapore and Toronto

Copyright © 1998 Reed Consumer Books Limited

A Catalogue record for this book is available from the British Library

ISBN 0 600 595994

Printed and bound in China

CONTRIBUTORS

1 GRAHAM VICKERS, architectural writer, speciality NYC, contributes to RIBA magazine and various books including Key Moments in Architecture.

2 CATHERINE MARCANGELI, NY-based art historian and writer. She has just completed her Doctorate in American Art History.

3 EMILY EVANS, fashion consultant and writer. Contributor for various successful fashion titles including the forthcoming Key Moments in Fashion.

4 NICK HARRIS, prolific author on cultural history whose writing includes works on the subject of American history.

5 LOUISE GUERIN, resident in NYC is a Brooklyn-based food writer, and has extensive first-hand knowledge of the subject.

6 HOLLY GEORGE-WARREN, journalist and editor for Rolling Stone magazine and author of several music books.

7 PATRICK CARROLL, written extensively about American sport, and is presently chairman of the Europe History Committee of the Society for American Baseball Research.

8 GARY VENA, NY theatre writer, author of 'Drama and Performance' and other books, lecturer in Theatre History at the Actors' Studio.

CONTENTS

8-31
ARCHITECT

Intrepid steel workers atop the 70-storey RCA Building in Rockefeller Centre get all the air and freedom they want by lunching on a steel beam with a sheer drop of over 240 metres (800 feet) to the street level – 1932.

Text: Graham Vickers

URE

t' Fort nieuw Amsterdam op de Manhatans

Architecture has always provided a highly visible link between past and present, but perhaps New York City demonstrates this phenomenon more dramatically than any other city on earth. Because its history as a great metropolis is comparatively short, New York's physical origins still clearly influence its present character and appearance. Despite significant changes in the city's fortunes, the past shows through, and in doing so it reminds us of the unique period of history in which New York City came into being. The city's neighbourhoods persist, often changing in character and purpose, but perpetuating the patterns of a rich – and sometimes explosive – racial and social melting pot. Most of all, its buildings, which are among the most monumental, optimistic, exuberant and daring ever erected, stand as a continuous and continuing testament to what Martin Amis has called 'the most violent thing ever done to planet Earth': New York City.

RIGHT Manhattan in the 1960s, with Battery Park in the foreground behind which towers the Financial District around Wall Street.

The extraordinary impact of New York's architecture defines the United States' most populous city not only for residents and visitors but also for millions of people who will never even go to America.

Some of New York City's most famous structures have become legendary icons, often epitomising the USA itself and becoming potent symbols of hope for generations of refugees, dreamers and fame-seekers.

For once, the reality proves to be as exciting as the illusion, even if first-time visitors are sometimes surprised to discover that some of New York's more celebrated buildings are easily missed in the dense surroundings of less familiar ones. Aggrandised by fame, Grand Central Terminal, the World Trade Centre, the United Nations buildings, the Empire State Building and Times Square are nonetheless working components of a real city where they all still have contemporary roles to play.

Although New York City is an assortment of neighbourhoods scattered throughout five boroughs, the popular misconception persists that 'New York City' and 'Manhattan' are synonymous. It is a misconception that architecture tends to reinforce. There are many notable buildings to be found in the

ABOVE LEFT An early 17th-century engraving showing the first colonial settlement of the isle of Manhattan, then known as New Amsterdam.

ABOVE By the late 19th century the City of New York had evolved – the grid street layout can be clearly seen, as can Central Park in the far distance.

NEW YORK CENTRAL BUILDING

PARK AVENUE, NEW YORK

AT   THE   GATEWAY   TO   A   CONTINENT

city's total area of 787 square kilometres (304 square miles), but they are often widely scattered. It is in the constrained area of Manhattan Island (just 57 sq.km, 22 sq.mile) that most of New York's most memorable architecture is conveniently concentrated.

Vulgarity and grandeur, follies and monuments, heroic feats of engineering, tacky short-term developments, inspirational vanities and stunningly beautiful monoliths – New York has them all. Each has its reason for being there and each reason is rooted in the city's traditions.

HERITAGE & CHANGE

The city's composite picture changes on an almost daily basis as a result of an ingrained 'put 'em up/tear 'em down' building culture. Much of the traditional best – like Grand Central Terminal – has been saved. Some treasures – like the original Pennsylvania Station – have gone forever. For better or worse, change is built into New York's psyche, so the city that never sleeps is also disinclined to stand still. Building conservation was more

ABOVE An evocative poster from the 1930s showing the New York Central Building that stands over Grand Central Terminal.

RIGHT The magnificent interior concourse at the Grand Central railroad station with the cathedral-like effect of sunlight.

or less unknown until the 1960s, but – as
is so often the case in America – coming
to something late does not mean it cannot
subsequently be embraced with wholehearted
enthusiasm. No matter when you visit, New
York always seems to have more exciting new
and old buildings to see than any other
comparable strip of land on the planet.

ENLIGHTENMENT & INDUSTRY

Few visitors to Manhattan begin their
exploration in its northernmost reaches.
However, north of Harlem, Fort Tryon Park –
originally the C.K.G. Billings estate, donated
to the city by John D. Rockefeller, Jr – offers
an insight into the enlightened aristocratic
mentality that did so much to shape modern
New York. The park's centrepiece is an
imported group of French and Spanish
cloisters that houses the Metropolitan
Museum of Art's medieval collection.

In 1938 Charles Collens created this
unpromising-sounding architectural montage
from 12th- and 13th-century building
fragments, and then topped it off with a copy
of a French monastery tower. The result is an
unexpectedly successful hilltop building,

thoughtfully done with no hint of pastiche, and located in a way that makes you wonder if this is New York City at all. Rockefeller, in an astonishing complementary real estate gesture, purchased the view across the Hudson River as well. He restricted development there and as a result The Cloisters is not only a charming and approachable little museum annex in a pleasant Manhattan park, it also commands a fine Hudson River view beyond which a section of the New Jersey shoreline – The Palisades – is briefly transformed into an unspoiled stretch of woodland.

A little further south in Manhattan industrial reality takes over at the point where the George Washington Bridge connects the island to New Jersey. Of this fine suspension bridge the architect Le Corbusier said: 'Here, finally, steel architecture seems to laugh.' There is certainly a light-spirited feel to this enormously powerful and graceful bridge, designed and built between 1927 and 1931 by Swiss-born engineer Othmar H. Ammann, and still one of New York's great symbolic structures. When it was built its span of 1,067 metres doubled the existing record for suspension bridges. What it lacks today is the choice of vantage points that some of the city's other bridges enjoy, since there remain few places from which it can be seen unobscured. For this reason alone, the George Washington Bridge is an excellent reason for taking a boat trip around Manhattan. To pass beneath it is as impressive, in its way, as sailing under San Francisco's Golden Gate Bridge.

The George Washington's downtown companion piece, the Brooklyn Bridge, is more famous and was built between 1869 and 1893 in a truly epic construction programme littered with deaths, maimings, explosions, fire and fraud. Much praised when it was finally completed (by Washington Roebling who took over when his father John Augustus Roebling died after a construction-related accident) the Brooklyn Bridge seems to get even better with the passage of time. Today its promenade above the roadway – devised well over a century ago to relieve anticipated congestion in a crowded city – stands as an early recognition of a problem that many later building designers would have to address.

RIGHT A photograph from 1950 of the Brooklyn Bridge, with a dockhand shovelling coal by the pier.

RIGHT INSET An early 20th-century print of the Brooklyn Bridge showing the central walkway between two traffic lanes. The walk across the bridge is still a must-do for New Yorkers and visitors alike.

BELOW The Winter Garden in the Cloister of Saint-Guilhem, part of the medieval museum complex constructed in 1934–38.

PHOTOGRAPHIC PANORAMA OF NEW YORK.
View from the Brooklyn Tower.

A CITY FOR PEDESTRIANS

New York, like the Brooklyn Bridge, is best experienced on foot … as anyone who has sat imprisoned in its gridlocked traffic will confirm. The New York subway system, ugly and noisy but generally efficient, is the pedestrian's friend, making Manhattan and sections of the other boroughs accessible for exploration without a car. Gradually, respect for the pedestrian – whether office worker or tourist – has increased in New York, and one particular early architectural expression of this still stands as one of the world's truly great public spaces.

Rockefeller Centre is an unqualified success – a mixed-use midtown collection of soaring office towers, shops and leisure amenities conceived and built during the decade of the 1930s, forerunner of innumerable urban complexes the world over and still thrilling in its monumental scale.

Here a consortium of architects combined soaring office buildings, an ice rink, promenades, cafés, restaurants, stores and plazas in a midtown complex of 14 limestone buildings richly decorated with aspirational murals, mosaics, inlaid metal and wood veneer. All of its components continue to work well to this day. Radio City Music Hall lobby is almost certainly the most dazzling

BELOW The ice-skating rink – ever-popular with skaters and spectators – is a commanding feature of the central Plaza of the Rockefeller Centre, sunk below street level in front of the RCA (now General Electric) Building.

ROCKEFELLER

ABOVE The Art Deco neon of Radio City Music Hall, which has hosted live radio and television shows for decades, situated on the west ('Avenue of the Americas') side of the Rockefeller Centre at Sixth Avenue and 50th Street.

LEFT A shot taken in the 1930s of the amazing Deco lobby and Grand Staircase at Radio City.

CENTRE

example of Art Deco to be seen anywhere.
The ice rink remains a charming surprise
even when you know it is there. Meanwhile
the scale of the RCA Building still has tourists
craning backwards, disbelieving that anything
so user-friendly on the ground could possibly
rise so high into the heavens.

In that Rockefeller Centre building,
dominating all the other elements, is the
essence of New York's defining building
form: the skyscraper.

REACHING FOR HEAVEN

Manhattan is largely built on rock, which
of course offers an ideal foundation for tall
buildings. On such a small island the
skyscraper was a necessary form whose
realisation many believe to have sprung
from a sudden quantum leap in building
technology. This is not entirely the case.
In fact it was really the invention of the
passenger lift or elevator that made tall
buildings a feasible architectural form, and
the first safe passenger lift was installed in
New York City, at the Haughwout
Department Store in 1857.

With the new opportunity to build high,
architects were temporarily constrained by
the need to construct enormously thick
masonry walls at ground level in order to
support the much-increased building weight.
New York's Cast Iron Building of 1848
showed an alternative way ahead: a rigid
frame of iron could adequately support
increased upper-floor loads without making
an unattractive fortress of the building base.
The refinement of steel processing led to
frames that were lighter and stronger than
iron, and so even taller buildings were
possible. Zoning laws were passed to protect
city streets from becoming dark canyons,
and this would prompt a number of
restricted-height, stepped skyscrapers.
However, there was still plenty of room
for towering monuments, and technical
breakthrough was soon matched with some
grand celebratory architectural touches.

Many of those early skyscrapers can
still be seen in New York , often exceeding
in quality and proportion their numerous
taller successors.

The magnificent Woolworth Building of
1913 by Cass Gilbert, looked to the Gothic
style for its decoration. This was the dazzling

RIGHT The historic
Woolworth Building on
downtown Broadway, built
in 1913 as the head
offices of the Woolworth
retail empire and seen
here with the twin towers
of the World Trade Centre,
shrouded in mist, looming
in the background.

BELOW The rise and rise of
a skyscraper; occupying a
whole block, the Empire
State Building under
construction in 1931.

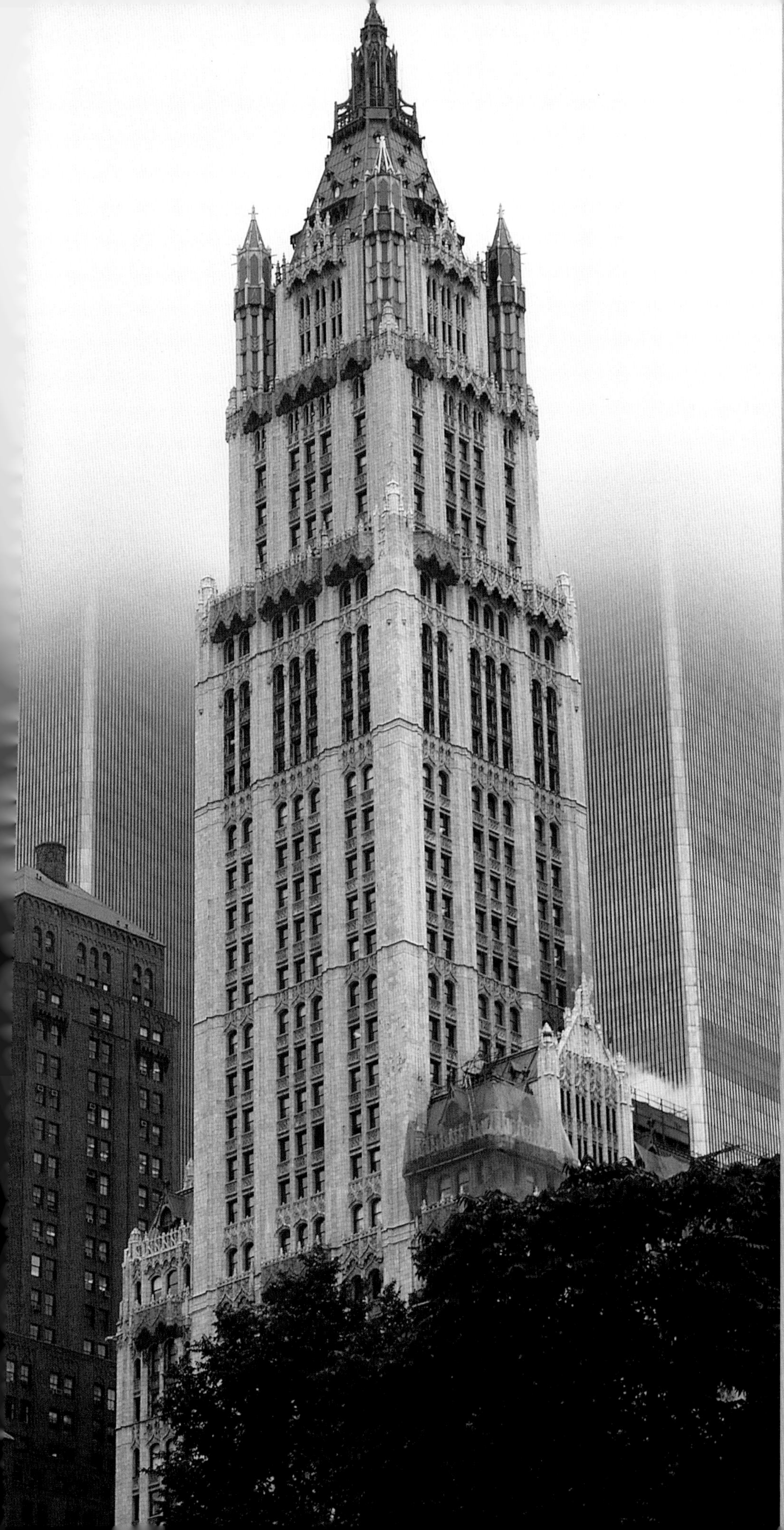

contemporary monument to retail success that Frank Winfield Woolworth wanted, and ironically the building was destined to outlast his hugely successful empire of five & dime stores. Woolworth finally closed their doors in the USA in 1997.

The 51-storey General Electric Building of 1931 (originally tenanted by RCA) embodied intricate Art Deco lacework masonry features, and a crown that glowed from within at night. Thoughtfully designed to sit adjacent to a very different building – the Byzantine church of St Bartholomew on Park Avenue – the General Electric Building managed the trick wonderfully well and still stands, now cleaned and restored to luminous external beauty.

TRADITION & EXPERIMENT

Much of New York's Art Deco experimentation was thought daringly modern in the 1930s. The General Electric Building, the Chrysler Building (1930) and the Empire State Building (1931) were at the time viewed as recklessly futuristic creations. Today they are usually seen as charmingly dated, or as old-fashioned predictions of a future that never came about. Even so, the effortless beauty of these buildings – not just of their decorative elements but also of their proportional harmony and the way they fit in with their neighbours – remains one of New York's finest legacies.

The Chrysler Building in particular ought by now to be comically out of style, with its gargoyles and outrageous metallic crown of automobile imagery. Instead it is one of New York's great enduring icons, popping in and out of view as you move though the canyons of the streets and avenues, reflecting the sun in the daytime and glowing with zig-zag neon strips at night in perpetual celebration of a brave automotive future. Once again, the monument has outlasted the dream: the building has changed hands several times; nowadays less of the cars in the traffic jams below are US-made; and greenhouse gas emissions are beginning to make America's love affair with the automobile look less heroic year by year. Perhaps for exactly those reasons, the Chrysler Building reminds us of architecture's power to evoke and celebrate, through its permanence, the transitory nature of human dreams.

LEFT The epitome of Art Deco splendour, the Chrysler Building, with its 'hub caps' and other automobile-inspired decorative features.

BELOW Though not the tallest building in town anymore, after the Statue of Liberty the Empire State Building is probably New York's most famous architectural landmark.

The New York skyscraper's development was abruptly changed by the ascendancy of the International Style. The notion of unadorned simplicity that came through the influence of a handful of émigré European architects and designers (led by Gropius, Breuer and Mies van der Rohe) resulted in a clutch of post-war monoliths, typified in New York by the Seagram Building of 1958.

Partly to moderate the impact of these sheer towers, a new set of zoning ordinances was brought in to stimulate the creation of more public spaces – plazas, parks and gardens – at street level. The Citicorp Centre (1978), by Hugh Stubbins Associates, was one of the models for the later breed of skyscraper/mixed-use sites, often brought about through a combination of land deals and enlightened architectural thinking. Sometimes those plazas became little more than windswept yards and these continue to pose a challenge to anyone who seeks to make them more convivial places – the famous twin tower World Trade Centre (1977) being a notable case in point. In general, though, New York has been successful in encouraging lively public spaces for shopping, dining and recreation.

As the perceived sterility of the brave new Modernist skyscrapers began to make a new generation of architects long for the exuberance of the Chrysler and Empire State Buildings, a "Post Modern" movement (mainly critical) emerged, advocating a return to some of the celebration and decorative playfulness that preceded Modernism. New York's primary built example of this trend was Philip Johnson's AT&T Building (1982), with its outrageous Chippendale chest of drawers impersonation.

Postmodernism spans many disciplines and enjoys many definitions, most of them imprecise. At its simplest it suggests a kind of knowing reference to the past that is neither pastiche nor slavish copy – a quotation from what has gone before that is meant to suggest both continuity and stylistic sophistication. By this definition much of New York's newer building programmes have Postmodern overtones. Meanwhile the city has at least one working monument of such quality that there was absolutely nothing to be done with it except to renovate it, clean it and admire it all over again.

RIGHT Built in Paris by the sculptor Frédéric-Auguste Bartholdi and shipped to New York in separate pieces, the Statue of Liberty was unveiled to the world in October 1886. Inscribed on its base are the immortal lines: 'Give me your tired, your poor, your huddled masses yearning to be free.'

BELOW The World Trade Centre on the lower westside of Manhhattan, for a time the tallest building in the world.

ABOVE Recently restored to its former glory, the concourse of Grand Central Terminal is once more a meeting place for all to enjoy, as well as an embarkation point for railroad passengers.

RIGHT The interior of the Oyster Bar in Grand Central Station. With its dramatic arches and decorative brickwork, it is a popular place to eat for New Yorkers and visitors alike.

A THOUSAND DRAMAS DAILY

Grand Central Terminal almost disappeared in the same wave of destruction that took the original Pennsylvania Station, an outstanding building whose design was in part based upon the Baths of Caracalla. Only last minute intervention by the Supreme Court in 1978 saved Grand Central from the same fate.

Completed in 1919 Grand Central became not only a great railway terminal (also, technically, a station for some of its through lines), but also an imposing public space for a great city. The logistic complexity of Grand Central's multi-level tracks and its interfaces with the road system and sidewalks outside stands as testament to a great piece of civil engineering. However it is the main concourse, a huge imposing space, that commands the attention of the visitor. Wildly romantic, with its arched windows, famous central icon of kiosk and clock, and stylised astrological ceiling decoration, it also has a cathedral-like quality that openly celebrates the early glamour of rail travel.

In fact a 1940s CBS radio show used Grand Central as the title and dramatic focus for its stories of 'a million private lives', casting the great building as an urban stage upon which were played out 'a thousand dramas daily'.

Today Grand Central is almost entirely unnecessary as a rail terminal. Commuter trains use it, and it has a related subway stop, but most heavy rail traffic has transferred to the mediocre modern-day Pennsylvania Station that lurks beneath Madison Square Garden a dozen or so blocks away. Here, though, is a tradition of New York that has been triumphantly reinvented. Grand Central has been sensitively revamped and cleaned. Unsightly billboards have been removed, public and private events are held there, cafés and shops have been upgraded and the overall result has been one of delightful rediscovery. Grimy chandeliers in the main waiting room revealed themselves to be gold. The murky ceiling was cleaned up to a surprisingly lively shade of blue. As Jeanne Giordano, the woman who co-ordinated much of the refurbishment work, remarked during the long 'cosmetic' renewal programme: 'The building really has great bone structure.' Still a great public building, Grand Central shows New York at its best.

NEIGHBOURHOODS

Architecture is not simply about monuments and monuments are not always architecture. The Statue of Liberty is a cliché that every visitor to New York should experience. It is an oddity, but an oddity that cannot fail to impress. It is a structure designed on another continent and planted in New York Harbour and yet it remains one that touches the same chords in the viewer as a great building does. The Empire State is both working building and monument, holding the street line remarkably well at ground level, and fully qualifying as a fine piece of architecture as well as a tourist trap with a fabulous view from the top.

These and a dozen other well-known landmarks each hold their own fascination, but they do not tell anything like the whole story of New York City's architectural traditions. This is found in the collections of buildings that form the neighbourhoods and the way the city's changing fortunes have obliged those neighbourhoods to adapt. The Fulton Street fish market evolved into a visitors' complex that, along with Boston's Faneuil Hall, set the pattern for many similar international exercises – Covent Garden in London and the Pompidou Centre in Paris, for example. The meatpacking district is

BELOW LEFT One of the architectural clichés of New York is the ubiquitous criss-cross of fire escapes down the side of buildings; these wrought-iron steps and balconies are in the downtown SoHo district.

BELOW RIGHT A traditional residential block in the Brooklyn Heights area.

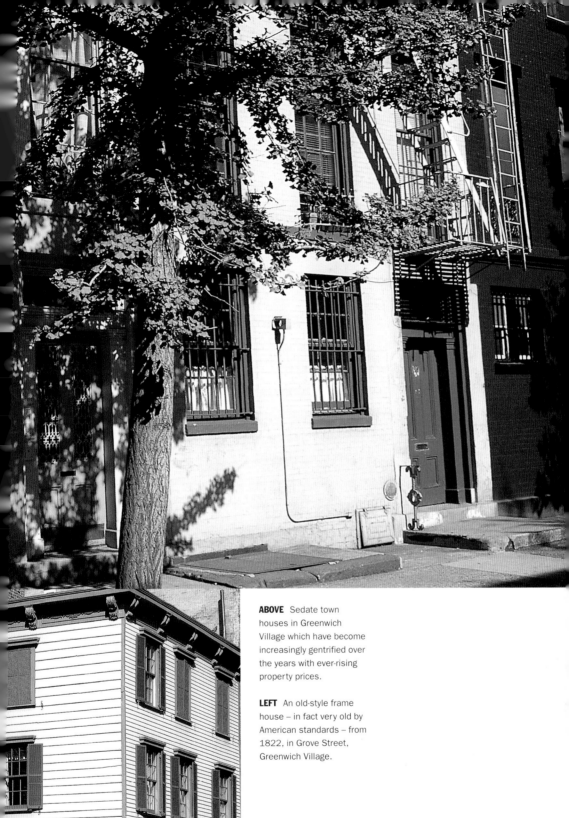

ABOVE Sedate town houses in Greenwich Village which have become increasingly gentrified over the years with ever-rising property prices.

LEFT An old-style frame house – in fact very old by American standards – from 1822, in Grove Street, Greenwich Village.

slowly changing to accommodate new industries, including film and video companies. The west side of *West Side Story* fame was summarily obliterated to make way for the Lincoln Centre arts complex.

Harlem, once a highly gentrified area, became a legendary black ghetto and still continues to reconfigure and adapt itself. Chelsea, Tribeca, Turtle Bay, Greenwich Village, Morningside Heights and a dozen other Manhattan districts all have a distinctive architectural flavour and individual street patterns. Battery City, a whole new business district, was tacked on to the lower part of the island by means of landfill. The famous theatres of 42nd Street degenerated into sleazy cinemas and sex shops and then succumbed to the Disney Organisation, who reinvented them for quite different – and considerably more 'wholesome' – entertainment purposes.

The fragmentary changes are also part of the story of New York's architectural tradition of adaptation, demolition and reinvention. Whatever charges may be levelled at it, New York can never be accused of becoming a museum of its own past. Nor, these days, can it be accused of being unmindful of its traditions. Architectural historians will always

BELOW Hosing the streets during a heat wave, to the delight of the local kids, among the poverty-stricken tenements on the Lower East Side, August 1922.

BOTTOM New York's 'huddled masses', typified by this immigrant family early in the 20th century.

bemoan the loss of this or that building, and often history will prove them right. However, New York was built upon action, aggression and ambition; it would be foolish to pretend otherwise or wish the built environment to shape the society it is meant to serve instead of the other way around. On the other hand, the city itself has slowly changed in character. It is no longer an industrial place and the forces that drive it are very different today from those of a century ago. Demographics have changed, service industries have grown, the suburbs have expanded and New York seems always to be on the brink of bankruptcy. As always, the architecture provides a living commentary to events.

Somehow, though, this extraordinary vertical explosion of brick, steel, concrete and glass is always more than the sum of its parts. It seems to mark out a charmed territory where people will always take risks, where energy never runs out and where virtually anything – good or bad – seems possible.

ABOVE Chinatown NY, where even the telephone booths are in character.

LEFT The Flatiron Building, known as such because of its wedge-like shape, was the first steel-frame skyscraper. When it was built in 1902, at over 91 metres (300 feet) it was the world's tallest.

LATIRON

Frank Lloyd Wright's architectural masterpiece with
spiral ramp walkways, the Solomon R. Guggenheim
Museum on 5th Avenue at 88th Street houses one of
the finest collections of modern and contemporary art.

Text: Catherine Marcangeli

ART 32-55

Art in New York? The word which springs to mind is 'profusion'. A very American tradition, philanthropy, has endowed the city with artistic institutions that have become its landmarks. The Fifth Avenue 'Museum Mile' echoes with the names of its benefactors: the Cooper-Hewitt Museum of Decorative Arts and Design was founded by Peter Cooper's granddaughters; the Solomon R. Guggenheim was designed by Frank Lloyd Wright – opened in 1959, it occupies an entire block on Fifth Avenue, and is at least as famous for its architecture as for its collection. The Metropolitan Museum, New York's answer to the Louvre or the British Museum, was not founded by a government or monarch, but thanks to private contributions, by the likes of J. Pierpont Morgan, William K. Vanderbilt or John D. Rockefeller, Jr. As for Henry Clay Frick, he was a collector very much in the vein of Jacquemart André in Paris: he first opened his mansion to the public in 1935 to display a museum-standard collection, but in a domestic, almost intimate setting. Across the East River, Sunday strolls in Brooklyn often lead to Prospect Park, the Botanical Gardens and the Brooklyn Museum; one of New York's major attractions, the Museum was initiated by yet another philanthropist, the distiller Augustus Graham, and its collection of Egyptian antiquities is among the finest in the world.

So, what is the place of the contemporary artist in a society where art has been seen as something bestowed on the community, rather like a hospital or a public library? Mrs Whitney left an endowment to provide for the Whitney Museum of American Art, founded specifically to exhibit living American artists; yet, in the words of art dealer Betty Parsons, 'If someone wants to see what's going on in art, he has to go to the galleries.' There, too, almost mythical names are associated with major episodes of recent American art: galleries and exhibition spaces – Stieglitz, Kootz, Janis, Frumkin, St Etienne, Pace, the Kitchen, Franklin Furnace; landmark exhibitions – the 9th Street Show, the Times Square Show; even the names of 'movements' relate to locations in the city itself – the New York School, the East Village Scene. In New York, art history is seen in terms of geography.

LEFT The magnificent Collonade Garden Court in the mansion housing the Frick Collection of old masters, classic French furniture and Oriental rugs.

ABOVE Art philanthropists LaGuardia, Rockefeller and MoMA director Barr.

BELOW LEFT The Whitney Museum features a permanent collection and special exhibitions of American art of all kinds.

BELOW RIGHT Also on the 'Museum Mile' of Fifth Avenue, New York's premier art gallery the Metropolitan Museum of Art – 'the Met'.

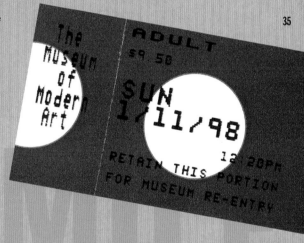

After World War II, the United States' political and economic power was matched by a new enthusiasm and confidence in the artistic field. During the 1930s, the art projects sponsored by the Work Progress Administration had attracted a great number of artists, writers, actors, dancers and musicians into the city; they were joined a few years later by an influx of European intellectuals and artists, refugees fleeing Nazism, such as Hannah Arendt, Mondrian, Leger, Breton, Ernst and Matta. By 1942, the WPA scheme came to an end, and artists began to find new outlets for their work.

The number of galleries had increased threefold over the war years, most of them to be found on the Upper East Side. Several galleries – McMillen, Peggy Guggenheim's Art of This Century and Betty Parsons – asserted their faith in young, unknown American painters like Jackson Pollock, an early exponent of Abstract Expressionism, by exhibiting them alongside the established French painters such as Matisse.

New York remains home to a multitude of galleries, many of them dating back to the war years. At 41 West 57th Street, beautiful 1930s elevators take the visitors through floor after floor of galleries. Only a few steps away, in 5th Avenue, eager tourists admire the windows at Tiffany's, many of them unaware of the wealth of art galleries nearby.

BELOW The innovative Art of This Century gallery, which was founded in the 40s by Peggy Guggenheim, with a radical design by Frederick Kiesler.

PEGGY GUGGENHEIM

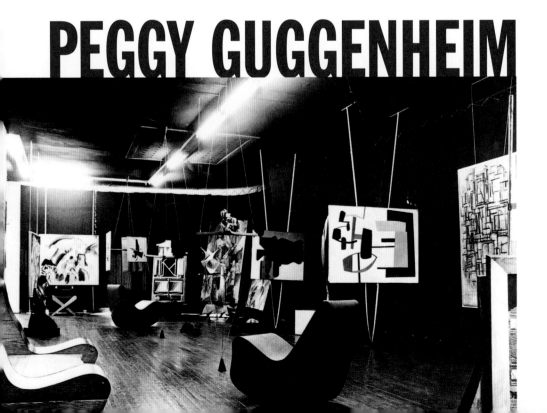

THE NEW YORK SCHOOL

Despite the influx of European artists, the New York School was soon regarded as truly American: its spontaneity, vitality, strength and independence were attractive to the new patrons of the prosperous post-war era. AbEx paintings were cheaper than the old masters collected by earlier philanthropists, and AbEx was chic: Pollock had been dubbed 'Jack the Dripper' by *Time* magazine in 1949, yet like works by Mondrian or Léger, his paintings were used in fashion photographs, in *Vogue* and *Harper's Bazaar*. Besides, the new movement was given the blessing of major critics Clement Greenberg and Harold Rosenberg; the involvement of publications, like *Art News*, and the support of Alfred H. Barr Jr, director of the Museum of Modern Art, gave Abstract Expressionism its needed credibility. Thanks to Barr, these paintings were shown at MoMA from the early 50s.

TOP The private view of the final show at the Tanager Gallery, an artists' cooperative gallery on East 10th Street, which closed in May 1962.

ABOVE Cecil Beaton's celebrated photograph for *Vogue* magazine in 1951, featuring a fashion model posed in front of a painting by Pollock and entitled 'Irene Before Jackson Pollock's Lavender Mist'.

POLLOCK

LEFT Director of the Museum of Modern Art Alfred H. Barr Jr, at an opening at the Museum in 1969; all of New York's high society would turn out, now art philanthropy had become 'smart'.

BELOW The Cedar Tavern in its 1950s heyday, the hang-out of the Abstract Expressionists and beat-writers. Closed in 1963, the Tavern can still be found on University Place, but not in its original spot.

CEDAR TA

The bar of the Cedar Tavern on University Place was the legendary haunt where the Abstract Expressionists drank, talked about art and fought over women. These days, poetry readings take place upstairs in the Tavern, now relocated to a nearby venue.

Downtown, Greenwich Village in particular, had long been associated with New York bohemia. In the early 1950s, a great number of artists, among them Wilhem de Kooning and Philip Guston, congregated in the area around 10th Street, attracted by cheap rents and spacious studios. With a can-do attitude still typical of New York artists, some of them began to rent storefronts or basements to open as cooperative galleries. The members shared the running costs, each showing in turn, with occasionally a group show including guest artists. The Friday night openings, generally advertised on bills posted around the neighbourhood (to save advance publicity costs), were social events which sometimes became street parties.

HAPPENINGS AND ENVIRONMENTS

Private galleries also mushroomed. The Reuben Gallery, on East Third Street, exhibited artists like George Segal, Red Grooms and Lucas Samaras, and provided the setting for environments and happenings by Allan Kaprow, Jim Dine and Robert Whitman. There, in his *Car Crash* happening, Dine, clad in an aluminium suit and wearing a headlight attached to a crash helmet, recreated a traumatic car accident.

In 1960, Oldenburg made *The Street*, an installation, complete with garbage and graffiti, recalling the decrepit buildings of New York's rundown neighbourhoods. In 1961, he opened The Store, on East 2nd Street: objects made of chicken wire and muslin, coated with plaster and painted with house-paint enamel, were 'for sale'. More than a setting or a subject, the city was becoming the very material of the art, and helped redefine what an artwork could be.

Discussions on art and politics took place in the galleries or in artists' studios. In the late 1940s, Franz Kline, Ad Reinhardt, Philip Pearlstein and others set up The Club, a forum which held Friday night discussions on topics ranging from 'Who owns space?' to 'What is the New Academy?', invited guest speakers and organised poetry readings. They

ABOVE An on-street art show in Greenwich Village, 1950. With then-cheap rents, which were perfect for painters seeking loft accommodation as studios, and cooperative gallery spaces, the Village soon became the centre of New York's art community.

VERN

also danced, drank and had fun.

The Club was walking distance from The Five Spot jazz club and, more crucially, from The Cedar Tavern: the management were accommodating when it came to cashing cheques or extending credit and there was (and still is) a board where odd-jobs and studio or loft vacancies were advertised. The Cedar, immortalised by Larry Rivers' series of *Cedar Menu* paintings, attracted artists, dancers, musicians and writers who lived or hung out in the neighbourhood. The Beats, especially Allen Ginsberg, who often attended the Club discussions, dropped in, as did the poet Frank O'Hara, whose *Lunch Poems* captured the magic of wandering through the city, like a modern-day Baudelairian flâneur.

These social contacts led to collaborations between artists working in different fields: Larry Rivers and Frank O'Hara (who also worked as an assistant curator at MoMA) produced a series of prints; John Cage, Robert Rauschenberg, Jasper Johns and later Frank Stella all collaborated with Merce Cunningham's Dance Company.

During the 60s, this tightly knit group gradually lost some of its cohesion. Uptown dealers had invited several artists to join their stables. New York was into its third generation of Abstract Expressionists, and what had been a movement had become a style. Some artists had died; others left the city, encouraged by the National Endowment for the Arts' policy of regionalisation. The scene imperceptibly shifted into new districts.

ABOVE Jim Dine in aluminium suit during his notorious happening 'Car Crash', at the Reuben Gallery in November 1960. Painter Robert Indiana can be seen in front of Dine.

BELOW Claes Oldenburg's happening 'Ironworks Fotodeath', staged at the Reuben Gallery in February 1961. 'Pop' painter Tom Wesselmann sits far left.

RIGHT New Year's Eve at The Club, 1958, a group that includes critic Harold Rosenberg (3rd left), painter Franz Kline (3rd right) and (2nd right) the 'beat' poet Ted Joans.

BELOW Merce Cunningham Dance Company in the 1958 'Summerspace', with choreography by Merce Cunningham, music by Morton Feldman and decor and costumes by painter Robert Rauschenberg.

THE CLUB

'FAMOUS FOR
FIFTEEN MINUTES

SOHO: 'FAMOUS FOR FIFTEEN MINUTES'

SoHo, the area South of Houston, down to
Canal Street, between Broadway and West
Broadway, constitutes one of the largest
groups of cast-iron structures in the world. In
the mid-60s, its abandoned manufacturing
lofts, often larger than the East Village
studios, were taken over by artists.

Around 1966, Warhol and his entourage
started frequenting Max's Kansas City, on
Park Avenue South. Many artists, poets and
musicians were already regulars; some even
had arrangements with owner Mickey
Ruskin, and could exchange their tabs for
paintings and sculptures. When Ruskin
opened another bar in SoHo, St Adrian's
Company, on Broadway and Third Street,
the same arrangements applied: the version
of Franz Hals' *The Guild of Saint Adrian* by
photorealist painter John Clem Clark not
only gave its name to the bar and hung on
the wall, it also kept Clark well provided
with food and drink. Fanelli's was no longer
the only SoHo artists' bar; later came the
Spring Street Bar, the Prince Street Bar and
a host of others.

And galleries, again, followed. Paula
Cooper opened a gallery in 1968, showing
minimalist and conceptual art, films,
performances, dance, poetry and music
events; the same year, Holly Solomon opened
the 98 Greene Street Loft, as a combined
exhibition and performance space. In 1969,
Ivan Karp, for ten years Leo Castelli's right-
hand man, opened O.K. Harris in an
enormous abandoned warehouse on West
Broadway; and Leo Castelli, who represented
Rauschenberg, Johns, Lichtenstein,
Oldenburg, Rosenquist and Warhol, moved
to SoHo in 1971.

Promotion was an essential part of the
scene. With characteristic cheek, Warhol
remarked that to be successful, artists need to
show in a good gallery, for the same reason
that 'Dior never sold his originals from a
counter in Woolworth's'. Indeed, the new
collectors – many industrialists and corporate
executives among them – had to be won
over; one of the keenest collectors of Pop,
New York insurance broker Leon Kraushar,
bragged: 'These pictures are like IBM stock,
don't forget that, and this is the time to buy,
because Pop is never going to die. I'm not
planning to sell my IBM stock either' – a far

LEFT The Andy Warhol
Factory entourage which
included 'superstars' like
Viva, Ultra Violet, Edie
Sedgwick and the actor
in many of the Factory
movies, Joe D'Alesandro.

BELOW A sale of Warhol
soup cans at Max's
Kansas City before it
became a punk club.

BOTTOM Max's in its
crowded heyday in 1966,
with paintings on the wall
that were payment in lieu
of bar tabs and restaurant
bills. Max's in the late 60s
was famous for its happy
hour, at which customers
could partake of
substantial free food for
the price of a beer.

43

TOP Action at the Factory as Andy Warhol gets behind the film camera, October 30, 1965.

ABOVE A card announcing Andy Warhol's Republique perfume window display at Bonwit Teller's department store in 1955. The design director was Gene Moore.

cry from dentist Meyer Pearlman who, a few years earlier, had acquired pictures by Tenth Street artists in exchange for dental services!

Throughout the 60s and 70s, groups of artists and intellectuals did address political issues and social problems. The Minimalist and Conceptual artists, though often perceived as remote and austere, were heavily involved in the Art Workers Coalition's protests against the Vietnam War. But the highly visible Pop scene did not appear as a locus of counterculture: Warhol or Lichtenstein did not fit the cliché of the estranged artist suffering in his garret; Rauschenberg, Warhol and billboard painter Rosenquist had designed window displays at Tiffany's and Bonwit Teller's. In 1962, in its deadpan idiom, Lichtenstein's *Masterpiece* posed the question of art as commodity while being itself a commodity; in 1966, Lichtenstein was producing dinnerware designs available by mail order.

Nor was the new avant-garde a members-only club, where artists looked mainly to their peers for approval. It reached a wide and varied audience. In 1966, Warhol organised a series of events with the Velvet Underground, The Exploding Plastic Inevitable, at The Dom, a club on St Mark's Place. 'Come and Blow your Mind', read the *Village Voice* ad. Artists (including Dali on one occasion), the drugged, the rich and the trendy danced to this multi-media show of music, slides, lights and film.

The SoHo scene, with its loft parties and club culture, became trendy; as gentrification progressed, SoHo started to become a

BELOW 'Masterpiece' by
Roy Lichtenstein, 1962.
Lichtenstein's comic book-
inspired paintings had a
sense of social satire
running through them –
and the New York art scene
was a perfect target.

ABOVE Andy Warhol operates the lightshow at a 1966 Dom performance by The Exploding Plastic Inevitable, the pioneer event that led to the multi-media rock music presentations of the 60s.

RIGHT A banner advertising The Exploding Plastic Inevitable outside the Dom on St Mark's Place, Greenwich Village.

FAR RIGHT The Velvet Underground spawned new areas in the collaboration of art and rock, with the experimental music of John Cale (foreground), Lou Reed's acerbic vocals and the accompanying Plastic Inevitable lightshow.

showcase for tried and tested art which had
originally emerged from alternative venues.

Today the scene in SoHo is one of relaxed
success. Music pours out of the recently
opened Guggenheim Downtown, everyone
ambles from gallery to gallery – this is the
new art establishment.

In Mercer Street, Japanese restaurants
and tap-dancing schools have opened next to
bars like Finelli's Café, where the Abstract
Expressionists once drank and talked.

ALTERNATIVE SPACES

In the 70s and early 80s, the East Village
was to become the centre of a new artistic
community: young, in-your-face and keen to
bypass the established market circuits. Their
productions ranged from graffiti, with artists
like Futura 2000, Keith Haring or Jean-
Michel Basquiat (tag: SAMO, short for Same
Old Shit) to Mike Bidlo's conceptual hand-
painted replicas of masterpieces.

Among second-hand and junk shops,
storefronts and dilapidated buildings were
again turned into galleries. The New York

State Council on the Arts' grants provided funds for non-profit exhibition spaces like Artists Space, which showed Laurie Anderson, Jonathan Borofski, Barbara Kruger and David Salle. Soon after, private galleries moved in: Fun Gallery, Nature Morte and Civilian Warfare, among others. Shows were also organised in local night-clubs – Club 57 on St Mark's Place, or the Limbo Lounge on 10th Street – and the artists mingled with local bands such as Blondie, The Ramones or poet-singer Patti Smith.

Other non-profit venues opened in other parts of New York City: The Institute for Art and Urban Resources aimed to transform abandoned New York buildings into exhibition, performance and studio spaces for contemporary artists. It now operates an empty school building in Long Island City, Queens, and The Clocktower Gallery in TriBeCa (the Triangle below Canal).

In the South Bronx, Fashion Moda, a store-front gallery, was created to give local artists the opportunity to exhibit and introduce the arts within deprived communities. In 1979, John Ahearn moved up to the South Bronx and collaborated with Puerto Rican artist Rigoberto Torres. The South Bronx Hall of Fame is an exhibition of

ABOVE South Bronx teenagers playing in front of a John Ahearn and Rigoberto Torres mural/sculpture 'Homage to the People of the Bronx: Double Dutch at Kelly St – 1981-1982'

ABOVE The Keith Haring Shop in New York sells T-shirts, posters and such featuring the characteristic graphics of the late Manhattan artist.

RIGHT The poster for the movie 'Basquiat', directed by Julian Schnabel with Jeffrey Wright playing Jean-Michel Basquiat and David Bowie as Andy Warhol.

ALTERNATI

JEFFREY WRIGHT

DAVID BOWIE

DENNIS HOPPER

GARY OLDMAN

MICHAEL WINCOTT

BENICIO DEL TORO

CLAIRE FORLANI

COURTNEY LOVE

PARKER POSEY

BASQUIAT

MIRAMAX INTERNATIONAL AND JON KILIK PRESENT A PETER BRANT JOSEPH ALLEN PRODUCTION A FILM BY JULIAN SCHNABEL DAVID BOWIE DENNIS HOPPER GARY OLDMAN JEFFREY WRIGHT "BASQUIAT" BENICIO DEL TORO CLAIRE FORLANI MICHAEL WINCOTT CASTING BY JOHN DUNN MUSIC BY DAN LEIGH PRODUCED BY RON FORTUNATO DIRECTED BY MICHAEL BERENBAUM EXECUTIVE PRODUCERS PETER BRANT JOSEPH ALLEN BASED ON A SCREENPLAY BY LECH J. MAJEWSKI PRODUCED BY JON KILIK SIGURJON SIGHVATSSON RANDY OSTROW WRITTEN AND DIRECTED BY JULIAN SCHNABEL
SOUNDTRACK AVAILABLE ON ISLAND RECORDS ℗ FEATURING MUSIC BY TOADIES, PJ HARVEY, TRACY BONHAM, GRANDMASTER FLASH AND OTHERS

28 MARCH

VE SPACES

ABOVE Walter De Maria's
'The New York Earth Room,
1977', an installation at
the Dia Centre for the Arts,
New York City.

Members Guide

P.S.1

P.S.1 Contemporary Art Center 22-25 Jackson Ave at 46th Ave Long Island City, New York 11101 t: 718.784.2084 f: 718.482.9454 e: mail@ps1.org

life-size figures cast from people living in the Black and Hispanic neighbourhoods around Walton Avenue. Here we can see little girls who have never been to The Cloisters or the Met skipping rope under sculptures of themselves. Like the work of Tim Rollins and K.O.S., this offers a new concept of public art, whose radicalism lies less in its form than in the context of its making. Ahearn and Rollins also show in 57th Street or SoHo galleries, while striving to preserve their integrity as socially aware artists.

Some artists embraced the swirl of the 80s art market. In 1980, The Times Square Show took place in an abandoned massage parlour, and received positive media cover. The thrill of illegal graffiti and East Village-type provocation was soon tamed on gallery walls: in 1985, Basquiat was making the cover of the New York *Times*, his paintings were selling for thousands of dollars and he was collaborating with Pop icon Andy Warhol.

Meanwhile, others chose to criticise aspects of the art world from within: Barbara Kruger's images and texts are printed on postcards, T-shirts and diaries, as well as in powerful installations; and, at a time when what little state support for the arts there was is being eroded, Hans Haacke makes us aware of the weight and motivations of corporate sponsorship, with its public relations and tax relief benefits.

Like all vibrant art scenes, these tensions between the established and the renegade are what makes it tick: Kruger and the Guerrila Girls are as NY Art as MoMA and the Met.

ART

51

NEW YORK CITY

BELOW Murals abound in New York City, as community-based political propaganda, free advertising and simply popular art. Those shown here are part of an Arts Project on 42nd Street.

PLUS CA CHANGE

Museums are part of the fabric of New York City: people go to MoMA to look at Monet's *Waterlilies*, watch a film, attend a debate or just sit in the sculpture garden. They take the elevator to the top of the Guggenheim and walk slowly down its spiralling ramp. The Whitney Biennial remains the show New Yorkers love to hate. And the art scene keeps moving.

A glance at the *Gallery Guide* street plan is enough to give a measure of the enormous range of choices available to the 100,000 tourists who amble through the streets of SoHo at the weekend: from outsider art to mainstream, via aborigines and Neo-Geo. Nor is there any shortage of debate: Artforum has, for instance, sponsored Lecture Series at the Drawing Centre, with such eminent critics as Yves-Alain Bois and Arthur Danto debating the sempiternal question of 'the death of painting'.

Yet, in the last few years, NoHo (North SoHo) seems to have been taken over by retailers, and rising real estate prices have forced some galleries out. Mary Boone closed her West Broadway Gallery in 1996 and moved uptown to 57th Street, saying: 'I just feel that if I'm going to be in the midst of retail, I'd rather be in the midst of retail I like.' New, smaller galleries are opening below

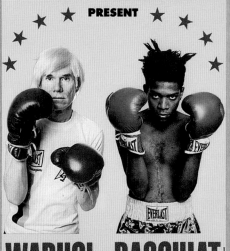

LEFT A 1985 poster published by the Tony Shafrazi Gallery in the West Village, advertising a joint exhibition of work by Warhol and Basquiat.

RIGHT Barbara Kruger created protest statements about the nature of art and its commercial aspects; the photograph 'Untitled (When I hear the word culture I take out my checkbook)' (138" by 60") appeared in 1985.

Broome Street (SoSoHo!), while some established galleries, like Paula Cooper, are moving to the developing 'Gallery Row', on Chelsea's 22nd Street, near the influential Dia Foundation art centre.

As for the artists, Manhattan prices have driven a great number to the boroughs; many now live and work in converted warehouse spaces in Williamsburg, and trendy bars and restaurants have opened round Bedford Avenue there. A group of artists are colonising Dumbo (Down Under Manhattan Bridge Overpass – New Yorkers definitely have a thing about acronyms …), though the area is still felt to be quite dangerous. In Long Island City, PS1 opened a new gallery in 1997, which will probably attract an artistic community.

In Manhattan Transfer, one of Dos Passos' characters is in perpetual search of 'the centre of things'. In the New York art world, notions of centre and periphery seem to lose their meaning, and traditions have less to do with stability than with movement.

LEFT The streets of New York, particularly in downtown Manhattan, are littered with graphic art of every kind imaginable.

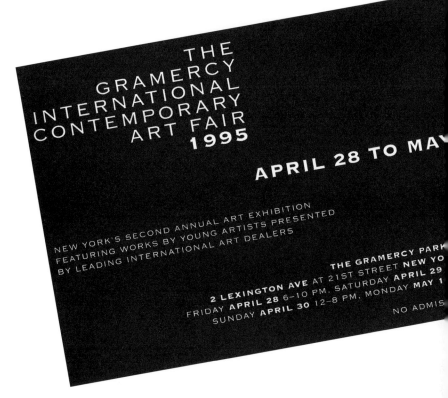

THE GRAMERCY INTERNATIONAL CONTEMPORARY ART FAIR 1995

APRIL 28 TO MAY

NEW YORK'S SECOND ANNUAL ART EXHIBITION FEATURING WORKS BY YOUNG ARTISTS PRESENTED BY LEADING INTERNATIONAL ART DEALERS

THE GRAMERCY PARK
2 LEXINGTON AVE AT 21ST STREET NEW YO
FRIDAY APRIL 28 6-10 PM. SATURDAY APRIL 29
SUNDAY APRIL 30 12-8 PM. MONDAY MAY 1
NO ADMIS

BELOW One of the best-known pieces of propaganda by the Guerrilla Girls, the New York-based agit-prop group exposing the art establishment from a militant feminist – and humorous – standpoint.

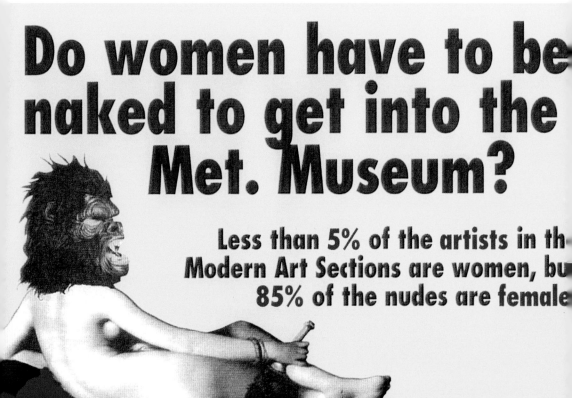

Do women have to be naked to get into the Met. Museum?

Less than 5% of the artists in th Modern Art Sections are women, bu 85% of the nudes are female

56-75
FASHION

Text: Emily Evans

The garment district in the 1950s; since the first large-scale waves of immigrants settled in New York at the beginning of the 20th Century, the city has been at the centre of clothes manufacture as well as fashion style.

F ashion in New York is firmly rooted in the simplicity of American style, a style born out of the post-Revolution need to rely on homegrown and homesewn clothes. Self-sufficiency was something encouraged by George Washington and religious groups such as the Amish and the Quakers. Ostentation was frowned upon in a nation keen to emphasise its democratic structure, and simplicity represented a strong survival instinct that Americans saw as the ultimate virtue. This influence has pervaded all of New York fashion history.

HOME SE

OME GROWN

American fashion for the masses did not really develop until World War II, which is when New York designers rose to prominence. The original principles of American style were the major influence and designers chose to diversify in a manner that still reflected where they had come from. NY fashion to date is ultimately identifiable in this respect: with egalitarianism and uniforms being a major cultural influence, with omnipresent denim representing the homegrown spirit of American style, with outdoor pursuits influencing the birth of casualwear and with the inherent simplicity of American style fusing with modern-day dressing requirements in what we now know as sportswear. Layer on top of that New York's rich cultural diversity, plus a nod to the prom style of the affluent Southern states, and you have a basic understanding of where New York fashion is coming from.

LEFT Elizabeth Street, lower East Side, where hundreds of immigrant families did garment work in tenements like these.

RIGHT A Cloak and Suit shop, typical of tailoring businesses that sprung up on the lower East Side in the early 20th Century.

WN

EGALITARIANISM AND THE UNIFORM

America as a nation was built on prospecting and industry – with gold mining, coal-mining, rail and road building and steelworking all becoming the boom industries of the 19th century. A huge country, America's railroads needed to traverse the states and manual labourers everywhere worked on building the nation's transportation system. The hard labour required hardy clothing and H.D. Lee designed and manufactured overalls for industry. The Lee Union-All became a staple item for manual workers everywhere, the item being what we now know as the denim bib 'n' brace. Levi Strauss similarly designed and manufactured for the mining industries, and from 1860 onwards their 9-ounce serge de Nimes jeans were the standard uniform for gold prospectors and coalminers everywhere.

America's culture is grounded in the appeal of the uniform and this grew in the 1920s as the car industry exploded, with denim worn in factories across the land. But it was not until the late 1940s that this working uniform was adopted as a fashion uniform. The teenage revolution was about to happen across the states and as part of their rebellious

ABOVE Beehive hair-dos and shift dresses on the streets of New York City in the 1960s.

LEFT An illustration from a 1940s advertisement for Lee jeans and overalls.

RIGHT Teenagers in New York's Chinatown in the 1950s, with *de rigeur* casual bomber jackets, T-shirts and slacks.

stance they adopted the blue collar staples of the workplace and made them sexy via T-shirts and leather jackets. This basic combination of jeans and T-shirt now represents the most egalitarian of Western fashion statements. Levi jeans, with their original styling intact, are still the most authentic jeans of choice in pulling together the look, and advertising campaigns reflect the history of the brand and its workaday appeal. The generic retail brand GAP promotes the ultimate in egalitarian chic with its basic jeans and T-shirt often modelled in ads by glamorous celebrities. This philosophy in dressing really is at the heart of American style and in particular New York style. More southerly states aspire to a less basic form of casual dressing but New Yorkers admire the authenticity and integrity of true basics. In addition, Casual Friday started in New York and liberated the office workers out of their uniform suits and into their more comfortable uniform of blue jeans.

The American fascination with uniforms does not end with jeans. US military uniforms of the 20th century came with much sexier styling than elsewhere, and the leathers of the air corps have inspired the rock 'n' roll uniform since the 50s (with the black leather bomber jacket and jeans of stars like Gene Vincent setting a precedent). The khakis of the ground corps have influenced an urban militant casual look, with khaki pants and shirts inspiring a 'thrift-style' street look that is very downtown New York, as well as designers such as Calvin Klein whose Khakis range is sold globally.

ABOVE The Gap store on lower Fifth Avenue, NYC.

BELOW British model Stella Tennant wearing a Ralph Lauren fringed jacket, photographed by Bruce Weber with a group of American boy scouts.

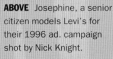

ABOVE Josephine, a senior citizen models Levi's for their 1996 ad. campaign shot by Nick Knight.

Other American uniforms feature in cult movies and simultaneously appear in designer collections across the globe. NY diner-style waitress uniforms came into focus in Quentin Tarantino's *Pulp Fiction* and then appeared in Stella McCartney's catwalk show. Likewise, the Mafioso New Yorker uniform of slim-fitting black suit, white shirt and narrow black tie that appeared in many a gangster movie of the early 90s, then cropped up in designer collections and magazine spreads around the world.

DENIM IN DESIGN

As well as offering a basic uniform to the world, the all-American denim jean continues to inspire designers everywhere into restyling, decorating and reviving this most basic item into something exclusive and eminently desirable. The commercial thinking behind designer-branded jeans is obvious: the exclusive designer endorsement of a product that everyone wears is a licence to print money! The concept began in New York in the mid-70s, with Gloria Vanderbilt designing glamorous jeans with trims and heavy branding for wealthy uptown Manhattanites, and was swiftly followed by

URBAN RANGERS

Calvin Klein in the late 70s with his infamous Brooke Shields ad campaign. Designer denim is now a feature on every catwalk, from Gucci in Italy to Katherine Hamnett in London, but New York is the homeland of chic jeans and Calvin Klein's Times Square oversize billboard featuring Kate Moss in CK jeans is the epitome of easy New York style.

URBAN RANGERS

The great outdoors, natural living and an adventurous spirit inspired the most rugged of all looks in American style and many New York designers, most notably Ralph Lauren, have come up with a version of American chic that incorporates low-cut jeans, leather accessories, slim-fit shirts and decorative belts – in a look that owes a lot to the cattle ranchers of the last century and to a time when the Rocky Mountains literally met Vermont. With a terrain traversing everything from snowy ranges to desert to subtropical beaches, outdoor pursuits are a major feature of American style.

The mountainous landscape and lifestyle have been a major influence on designers such as Ralph Lauren, with suede jackets, handknit sweaters and moleskin pants all featuring heavily in winter collections. For summer, resortwear offers inspiration to most New York designers and an insight into how Americans with money spend the warm, early months of the year in glamorous coastal resorts such as Cape Cod and Key West.

Early New York designers seized upon this as a major influence, the most notable of whom was Claire McCardell, the first New York ambassador of comfortable, sports-influenced fashion for women. She was once quoted as saying: 'Clothes that go with active sports show up your background more than any other clothes.' She paid particular attention to comfort, practicality and ease of care and she abhorred the idea of women being overdressed for outdoor pursuits. She became known for her playsuits and halterneck dresses and for her use of basic American fabrics like cotton corduroy and wool jersey. She inspired every NY designer to follow and resortwear is now a staple of NY style. There is an irony in that much of it is dressing for wealthy Americans who can afford to holiday in springtime, yet its fabrics

LEFT A billboard in the streets of Manhattan featuring Kate Moss in the 1994 Calvin Klein Jeans campaign.

BELOW Part of Ralph Lauren's fringed 'western' collection in 1989, inspired by America's fascination with its pioneer history.

and styling are super simple with cotton knits, easy shirts, cotton clamdigger pants and sailing shorts all being featured.

McCardell has particularly inspired young New York designers such as Isaac Mizrahi; and innovators like Calvin Klein have developed a new sports style thoroughly in keeping with modern dressing requirements that calls upon her use of simple shapes, performance fabrics and clean details in developing a new sportswear aesthetic. Zippered cardigans, soft pants, vest tops and all-in-ones are features of every American woman's wardrobe and are uniquely American in their inception. Yet now they inspire designer collections around the globe, with streamlined fashion leading us into the millennium.

While Ralph Lauren's ranch style offers a lifestyle statement for those drawn to the history and tradition of America's open country, the resort look owes more to the glamour of early 1950s socialites such as Babe Paley and C.Z. Guest. Both styles offer a little escapism from urban life into a world of play and activity, be it mountain walking or sailing!

ABOVE The ready-to-wear sportswear designer Tina Leser based this 1949 playsuit on the Japanese kimono look.

LEFT A zipped top from the Jill Sander catwalk show for Autumn 1977.

FAR LEFT Calvin Klein, reviving the full skirt and off-the-shoulder top, achieved a very retro-50s look in 1985.

ABOVE Power dressing from Donna Karan, from her Spring/Summer collection of 1986.

ABOVE The eight piece capsule wardrobe that Donna Karan introduced for Autumn/Winter 1986/7.

THE EIGHT-PIECE CAPSULE WARDROBE!

During the 1980s American designers took the simplicity ethic to its most extreme lengths. In an increasingly fast-moving world, where women were taking on more responsibility in the workplace, and occasionally in the boardroom, new demands were being made of designers in creating workable wardrobes. Power dressing was at the height of its popularity, women were dressing for success and more emphasis was being placed upon clothes that worked all day long – that could take the busy career woman from breakfast meeting to cocktail party. Donna Karan was the designer to come up with the ultimate in capsule dressing, creating an eight-piece wardrobe that rolled up into a piece of airline handluggage, that didn't crease and that offered flexibility through the day's varied schedule. The body and overlaying body blouse, the cashmere sarong, the formal jacket ... eight pieces that interacted in fulfilling a woman's total wardrobe requirements.

Although the concept of capsule wardrobing now seems slightly outmoded, the influence has been paramount in furthering the idea that American designers are the best at basics, and commercially viable designer collections around the globe all now feature a good high-quality basics range of their own making.

ABOVE Simple elegance comes to the fore with Donna Karan's evening outfit, Autumn/Winter '87.

KARAN

MANHATTAN GLOBETROTTERS

The rich cultural melting pot that is New York brings with it its own eclectic style that is entirely self-grown. Ethnic influences come to New York from around the globe via Manhattan's suburbs, with Hispanic communities, Afro-Caribbean districts, Little Italy and a strong Jewish contingent. Everything in New York is touched by this exciting diversity, particularly fashion.

New York street style is probably most heavily motivated by local black culture and trends, and in the past 20 years this has been driven by developments in true sportswear. Track and field apparel has always appealed to urban black youth, whose heroes often came from similar inner city areas to rise as stars of the sports world. This attainability led black kids to adopt the style of the locker room as their own, and sportswear status symbols soon gained momentum with each new product launch. Since the mid-80s this influence has pervaded New York street style generally, with the ceaseless switching from one new product to another appealing to fickle street-style sensibilities. In addition, the rise of the training shoe as a means for New Yorkers to get practically from A to B, means that sportswear is a major visual feature of the New York sidewalk.

Trends change fast, the ongoing war between Nike and Reebok often thrown into perspective by the sudden desire for retro 70s trainers, or a little-heard-of brand from Europe. The major sports brands now develop clothing ranges meant for the street, and designers have been swift to pick up on the demand for true sportswear with a hefty label. New York designer Tommy Hilfiger is currently the most successful of these, with the all-important backing of New York's rap stars throwing him into the global limelight as the name to wear.

ABOVE Tommy Hilfiger, sportswear supremo, with two of his models in October 1996

HILFIGER

ABOVE Kate Moss models
Tommy Hilfiger for his
Spring/Summer collection
of 1997.

RIGHT More New York
street ads – the phone
booth displays Kate Moss
for Calvin Klein's
Obsession perfume.

ABOVE A mural for Donna Karan dominates this New York street scene.

Fashionable New Yorkers mix this major sportswear influence with other features of the city's visual make-up. They take the glitz of the Hispanic community, some thrift items from the downtown flea markets and go back to the black district for some authentic African accessories.

Designers such as Patricia Field and Xuly Bet (who is a Parisian settled in New York) have developed this eclecticism into a retail offering. Field's downtown store features different local designers' work – with showgirl-style mesh tops sitting next to rasta striped T-shirts and unusual branded sneakers. Other labels, such as Sofia Coppola's Milk and Kim Jacobs' X-Girl, mix the hi-tech influences of urban technology (in sci-fi logos and futurist fabrics) with the low-key influences of 70s Harlem.

New York street style is about as diverse as it gets. The locality of its influences – the ethnic suburbs, the downtown flea markets and the uptown designer stores – dictate this. Calvin Klein's diffusion range, Ck, reflects the melange (with his endorsement and a designer price tag), as does Donna Karan's DK sub-brand. Klein's famous jeans and underwear ads featuring Marky Mark in low-slung hipsters with the elastic of his boxers showing came straight off the streets of Brooklyn and Queens, where trousers were being worn oversized to show off designer undergarments. And while the original innovators on the street continue to find new things to put together (and new ways in which to do so) New York street style will continue to be a major influence on the way we dress.

ABOVE The Gucci store on Fifth Avenue represents one luxurious end of the fashion market

RIGHT Shopping for clothes at a more modest level, in one of New York's many street market sites.

TOP 1948 advertising for Saks of Fifth Avenue.

ABOVE 1949, a lady trying on hats at the newly-opened branch of the Bloomingdales store in Fresh Meadow, Queens.

RIGHT A 1948 ball gown by the costume designer Irene, a juxtaposed silk taffeta skirt and white underskirt.

PROM STYLE

While most of New York fashion can be identified by its simplicity and practicality, there is an area of design that harks back to the Southern Belle style of the last century, to Hollywood musicals of the 1940s and to a girly 1950s prom style that is just as American as blue jeans. The moneyed families of the Southern states in the last century offered up a completely different stylistic stance to the rest of America. The most extravagant of gowns imaginable asserted the affluence of the wearer and, in turn, inspired many a costume in Hollywood's epic musicals of the 1940s.

The new affluence of 20th-century America led to a demand for eveningwear and glamour on more of a mass scale than had been seen before, and the New York designers of the 1940s offered this in abundance.

One of the best known and most influential of these was a designer called Mainbocher, who had a Paris training but American roots. This combination of influences was an inspiration for many designers to come and was the mix that wealthy Americans loved. Mainbocher managed to combine a luxurious American practicality with the drama of Paris.

He designed superb ballgowns and very glamorous daywear but gave everything an American touch, such as making sweaters and cardigans for evening to be worn with taffeta gala skirts. Similarly, he juxtaposed fabrics like linen and silk – something a more traditionally driven Parisian would never think of doing. The lack of history in American design left Mainbocher at liberty to do this, and his legacy lives on via designers such as Calvin Klein, Donna Karan and Bill Blass. New York designer eveningwear often features such quirky juxtapositions – cashmere T-shirts from Donna Karan offer practical luxury, a simple twinset is combined with an extravagant jewelled skirt at Bill Blass and Klein's strapless cocktail dresses are cut from simple suiting fabrics.

Such is the spirit of New York fashion: without the mental boundaries imposed by history and tradition found in Europe, with all of the benefits of a multi-cultural social make-up and with a respect for the clothes of the working man which, far from being patronising, is heartfelt and very real.

FESTIVALS 76-95

Text: Nick Harris

RELIGION

The varied ethnic communities in New York have all brought their own faiths and festivals to bear on the culture of the City. Here a Harlem church congregation take part in a highly charged 'sanctified' gospel service.

I f America is a melting pot, New York City is the corner of the pot where the largest number of ingredients are concentrated – and go on bubbling furiously. People of the most diverse origins and faiths live here and make a point of maintaining their traditional customs, festivals, feasts, ceremonies and services. These may be assertions of an old and separate identity, but they often acquire a distinctively Big Apple flavour, and many of them attract other New Yorkers who love a show or a chance to sample a specialised cuisine. And since everybody joins in the nationwide celebrations of their shared Americanness, the calendar of this city of workaholics is crammed with more festivals and holidays than any single chapter could possibly do justice to.

One place to begin is with the quintessential American holiday, Thanksgiving, which is always celebrated on the fourth Thursday in November.

The festival commemorates the Pilgrim Fathers who, in 1620, sailed from England to Cape Cod in their ship the *Mayflower* and founded a first settlement at Plymouth, Massachusetts. Helped by their Native American neighbours, the settlers successfully sowed and harvested the crops, including Indian corn, which would see them through the coming winter.

The three-day feast that followed was the first Thanksgiving, at which the settlers were joined by 90 Native Americans and where thanks were rendered to God for the delivery of the harvest.

The Pilgrim Fathers were religious separatists – so-called 'puritans' who refused to conform to the Church of England – but the annual Thanksgiving was to become a national ritual, performed by people of all faiths who had settled and prospered in the New World.

LEFT A firework display illuminates the New York skyline during the 1986 July 4th celebrations of Independence Day.

BELOW The faithful carry candles during a Roman Catholic saint's day ceremony in the Little Italy district of lower Manhattan.

ABOVE A scene from the 1947 movie *Miracle On 34th Street* with Macy's Thanksgiving Parade on West 34th Street

RIGHT Macys, the 'world's biggest store' which organises the annual Thanksgiving Parade.

Modern Americans travel astonishing distances to be with their families at Thanksgiving, when the traditional meal of turkey, cranberry sauce and pumpkin pie is consumed around a table decked with ears of Indian corn. Ever since 1924 New Yorkers have started the day by taking their children into Manhattan for a special treat: the Macy Parade, mounted by the famous department store. Santa Claus puts in a welcome, if premature, appearance, and floats cruise along the road from the Natural History Museum at Central Park West to Herald Square, where Macy's itself takes up an entire block. The thrilling point of the proceedings is aeronautical – the huge rubber balloon models of Mickey Mouse, Donald Duck, Snoopy, Superman and more recent characters from cartoons and comics that float, helium filled, above the throng.

Then, while the dinner is being prepared, many New Yorkers work up an appetite by some vicarious exercise, marking the climax of the college football season by watching the Army–Navy local encounter on television or, if the Army college team is playing at home, out at West Point.

HE MACY P

ABOVE A gigantic Betty Boop, typical of the huge inflated characters that are a main feature of the Macy's extravaganza.

CHRISTMAS

Thanksgiving is followed by a frantically observed day of shopping sales, which can be regarded as the first manifestation of the Christmas spirit. As in many other parts of the Western world, Christmas is celebrated by the secular as well as the religious, and even by people of other faiths who see nothing to object to in the decorated tree, Santa Claus, present-giving and other general jollities.

New York's Christmas traditions predictably tend towards the spectacular, with Fifth Avenue very much to the fore. The Christmas decorations along its length are legendary, and every year lavish, ingenious animated window displays draw crowds for weeks to big stores such as Lord and Taylor, Saks Fifth Avenue and Bergdorf Goodman's. At the beginning of December an enormous Christmas tree is mounted in front of the 70-storey GE (formerly RCA) Building inside the city-within-a-city that is the Rockefeller Centre, and thousands of people come to watch the ceremonial lighting-up. Churches all over the city put on concerts as well as

ARADE

ABOVE The statue of Prometheus at Rockefeller Plaza, with Christmas tree in the background.

BELOW The Rockefeller Plaza with Christmas tree and angels as viewed from Fifth Avenue.

services, and at New York's great cultural complex, Lincoln Centre, the Messiah Sing-In gives those who would normally be in the audience the chance to rehearse and perform Handel's great oratorio.

Annual fare of a very different kind is on offer in the Christmas spectaculars at Radio City Music Hall. Now part of Rockefeller Centre, Radio City was born in 1932, during the heroic age of cinema architecture. Then, as now, the biggest indoor theatre in the USA and a masterpiece of Art Deco, it filled its 6,000 seats by combining film shows with variety acts, abetted by elaborate stage machinery, the 5-ton Mighty Wurlitzer organ and, not least, the high-kicking legs of its chorus girls, the Rockettes. After three decades as a New York institution, competition from TV and changes in movie distribution lessened the appeal of Radio City. By 1978 it was so run down that the management announced that it must close – at which point New Yorkers realised that they were losing a tradition and, after furious public protests, the decision was revoked. Radio City was restored to its former glory and its fortunes revived as a purely stage theatre with the production of ever more elaborate musical extravaganzas. Needless to add, the Rockettes remain an essential element in the Radio City tradition, so closely identified with New York that they are often lured away from the theatre to grace various public occasions.

ABOVE A January 1947 *Saturday Evening Post* cover showing the clearing up to be done after the New Year's Eve celebration in Times Square.

ABOVE Hasidic Jews in their traditional headgear walking children in New York's lower East Side.

Although Christmas commands wide loyalties, it is not without competitors. Each December, shops are stacked high with cards for three festivals which brighten the mid-winter scene: Christmas; Hanukkah, the Jewish Festival of Lights; and the African-American holiday, Kwanzaa.

HANUKKAH

There have been Jews in New York since 1654, long before the great 19th-century influx from Germany and Eastern Europe took place. American Judaism fostered a number of branches and sects, but the most important festivals continued to be observed in the home and at the synagogue rather than in public. The main exception is Hanukkah, an eight-day celebration which usually falls a week or two before Christmas. The festival commemorates the victory in 165 bc of Jewish heroes, the Maccabees, over the Hellenistic Syrian state, and the rededication of the Temple in Jerusalem. At home, Jews light a single candle on the first day, two on the second, and so on. But in New York they also go to Brooklyn's Grand Army Plaza, where a giant candelabrum is lit up nightly during the festival.

Although inspired by African harvest festivals, Kwanzaa ('first fruits') is a remarkable example of a recent, consciously created tradition whose popularity proves that it has satisfied a real need. It was devised in 1966 by a black studies professor, Dr Maulana Karenga, as an independent, secular holiday for African-Americans, lasting from 26 December to 1 January. Centred on family and community values, it involves the daily lighting of a candle in a seven-branched candelabrum, and comes to a climax on 31 December with a communal feast.

After the briefest post-Christmas lull, New Yorkers prepare to confront the magic moment when the Old Year ends and the New begins. Energetic souls assemble in Central Park, at the Tavern on the Green, for the 8-kilometre (5-mile) Midnight Run, while poets and verse lovers read in the New Year at St Mark's Church on Second Avenue. For a majority of New Yorkers, however, public celebration of New Year's Eve takes place in Times Square; most of them watch the junketings on television, but thousands pack the square to take a direct hand in the

BELOW Orthodox Jews in New York awaiting the start of an Orthodox parade.

BOTTOM Men dancing together at an Hasidic wedding. Women are present, but Hasidic Jews believe in extremely strict segregation of the sexes.

85

action. This particular tradition began on 31 December 1904, when the *New York Times* moved into the 25-storey building that became known as the Times Tower. Seizing the opportunity for city-wide publicity, the *Times* put on a midnight firework display – with such success that it became an annual event. In 1908 this barely established tradition was extended in a bizarre fashion when a 90-kilo (200-pound) sphere was lowered from the top to the bottom of the building's flagpole. The *New York Times* long ago moved around the corner to West 43rd Street and the tower has been renamed One, Times Square Plaza; but there is still a Ball Drop, and the moment when the countdown ends and the ball hits the bottom on the stroke of midnight is still the signal for frenzied rejoicing and the cutting of more or less alcoholic capers.

Daunting after the excesses of Christmas and New Year's Eve, New York's freezing Januaries hardly encourage the festive spirit. But the vagaries of history have placed Chinatown in Lower Manhattan, and the Chinese calendar lays down that the new year begins about the end of January. Chinatown began in the late 19th century as a tiny settlement around Mott Street, home to a bachelor population that was prevented by US immigration laws from bringing wives and children into the country. Surviving fears of the 'Yellow Peril', rumours about white slave trading and the all-too-real gang violence of the Tong Wars, the Chinese community established and enlarged itself. Now spilling over into Little Italy and the Lower East Side, Chinatown is one of the most exotic areas of Manhattan, a jumble of food stalls and curio shops, galleries, restaurants, garment factories and temples red

BELOW LEFT A common image of Chinatown – a gold shrine of the Laughing Buddha.

BELOW & RIGHT Chinese Americans celebrating the New Year in NYC's Chinatown with bright costumes and fantastical dragon dances.

CHINATOWN

and gold, where many people can still be found who speak little or no English. Chinese immigrants brought with them the three traditional and interlinked creeds of Confucianism, Daoism and Buddhism. Of these, the last has the most visible public presence, notably in the Eastern States Buddhist temple on Mott Street. Always thronged, Chinatown becomes even more densely populated during the New Year festivities, as Chinese from the outlying boroughs join the residents and the swarms of tourists. No one seems much concerned about anything but having a good time, irrespective of whether it is the Year of the Tiger or the rather less forbidding Year of the Hare, and the day goes off in a noisy, apparently chaotic succession of leaping, mythologically masked figures, parades, fireworks, dragons and kites.

ST PATRI

February is the month for most department store sales, somehow justified by being associated with the birthdays of George Washington and Abraham Lincoln. It is also, for even more mysterious reasons, when traditions have grown up around the Empire State Building. Every year a carefully vetted group of athletes assembles in the lobby for the Empire State Run-Up; they go right to the top, in the same ambitious (some might say vainglorious) spirit as the couples who choose to marry there on 14 February, St Valentine's Day.

ST PATRICK'S

In China, the New Year is the harbinger of spring. Not so in New York, however, whose residents must wait until March and hope that St Patrick's Day, on the 17th, will mark the turning point. The St Patrick's Day Parade is the first of an entire season of ethnic marches in New York City. Many of these parades are routed along Fifth Avenue, the great artery that runs from south to north through Manhattan, starting at Washington Square, passing the vast playground that is Central Park, and stretching all the way to Harlem. A single thoroughfare which can boast of taking in the Park, the Empire State Building, the Trump Tower, Cartier's, Tiffany's and the 'museum mile', Fifth Avenue represents the American Dream in its most grandiose form.

The first of New York's ethnic groups to assert that it had 'arrived' by marching down Fifth Avenue were the Irish-Americans; and the St Patrick's Day Parade remains not only the first parade of the season but the greatest and grandest. Its origins in New York City have been traced back to an inspired improvisation by Irish militiamen in 1762, but for much of the 19th century the parades in New York and elsewhere were held in defiance of widespread anti-Irish prejudice and malicious attempts to disrupt them. By the end of the century, however,

ABOVE The New York Irish community – and many more besides – take part in the annual 'St Pat's'

BELOW Commercial concerns have always been quick to get in on the act – here a recent Celtic Music promotion from a chain of Manhattan record stores.

89

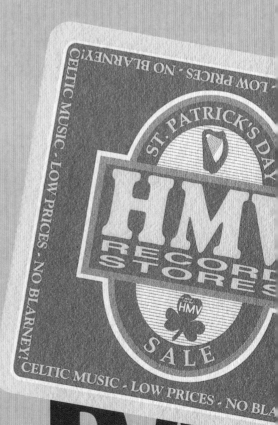

CK'S DAY

the Irish-Americans had achieved acceptance and the great new Gothic edifice of St Patrick's had been built on Fifth Avenue as the USA's first Roman Catholic cathedral, providing an obviously inviting focus for the proceedings held in the saint's name.

Lasting six hours or so, the parade is led by its Grand Marshal, escorted by mounted police and followed by members of the Ancient Order of Hibernians (which organises the event), the Emerald Societies of the New York City police and fire departments, war veterans, massed ranks of school-children and any other body of men or women which can secure acceptance for its Irish-American credentials. Only groups may take part in the parade and even such distinguished trespassers as Robert Kennedy and Jimmy Carter have found themselves escorted from the street. The blocks of institutional marchers are separated by large cruising floats, and by bands of varying sizes and ambitions piping an often eccentric selection of tunes.

St Patrick's Day commemorates a 5th-century British saint who was neither the first nor obviously the most successful

ABOVE The main Roman Catholic church in New York City, St Patrick's – in 1876 it stood alone, now the skyscrapers around Fifth Avenue dwarf it.

RIGHT The St Patrick's Day Parade – with pipers – passes St Patrick's.

Christian missionary to work among the pagan Irish. But somehow Patrick's personality left an indelible impression on the people, and he became their best-loved saint, as well as the official patron of the Emerald Isle. However, the St Patrick's Day Parade is more a celebration of Irishness than a religious occasion, and even the Irishness is of a peculiar kind. The fact is that huge numbers of New Yorkers consider themselves honorary Irish for the day and the entire city is saturated in green and is shamrock bedecked. The wearing of the green is the least of it: the white strip separating lines of traffic on Fifth Avenue is painted green for the parade; hair, faces, flowers and food are all emerald tinted; and at night on the 17th the Empire State Building is floodlit – in green.

A week after St Patrick's Day, Greek National Independence Day occasions another Fifth Avenue parade, with elegant traditional costumes and celebrations featuring the distinctive Greek style of dancing and cuisine. Cutting into the sequence of ethnic displays on the avenue, Easter provides the pretext for a mass

EASTER DAY PARADE

demonstration by New Yorkers who are – or who believe themselves to be – apostles of fashion. Midtown, from 44th Street to 59th, pedestrians have the avenue to themselves and fill it up from pavement to pavement. With TV cameras and journalists out in force for the Easter Parade, New York ladies saunter along with their escorts, showing the latest creations and flaunting often fantastical headgear that is hardly described by the traditional term 'bonnet'.

Then the ethnic parades begin again. Sunday after Sunday the drum majorettes twirl and toss their batons, the bands play, the marchers march, the floats float along. Among the best-known events are Martin Luther King Parade in May, honouring the memory of the great Civil Rights leader, and the exuberant, multi-band National Puerto Rico Day Parade in June. Two traditional ethnic parades that take place in late September or early October celebrate Von Steuben Day and Pulaski Day, respectively named after German and Polish heroes of the American Revolutionary War. A week later comes the parade for Columbus Day (12 October), now an essentially Italian-American occasion to commemorate the first sighting of the New World by the Genoese-born seafarer who led a three-ship Spanish expedition across the Atlantic in 1492.

BELOW The traditional Easter Parade – with the appropriate bonnets – on Fifth Avenue at the turn of the Century

Not all the Fifth Avenue parades are ethnic based: in late June, for example, there is a parade down to Washington Square as part of Lesbian and Gay Pride Week. Neither are all the parades confined to booked-up Fifth Avenue or even Manhattan, since every group from Norwegians to West Indians feels the need to assert its identity somewhere and at some time in the year. Often, the parade is reinforced or replaced by a carnival or a street festival, a much-favoured form of celebration that keeps a neighbourhood thronged – and its shops and stalls profitably busy – for days or, in the case of Harlem, a full week. Eating plays a large part in this kind of festival-going, so it is not surprising that, late in May, Ninth Avenue hosts a two-day Food Festival in which the culinary achievements of all New York's communities are on view and on sale for the thousands who visit it.

Of all the community festivals, however, the most popular still takes place over ten days in Little Italy, a focus of nostalgia despite the encroachments of Chinatown and the growth of Italian-American communities in other parts of New York. The mid-September Feast of St Gennaro honours the South Italian saint whose blood, preserved in a glass phial in Naples Cathedral, is said to liquefy at regular intervals. In Little Italy an effigy of

ABOVE Participants in the Easter Parade still wear the most creative of hats – here a flowery number from the 1997 event.

BELOW Brooklyn is the location for the biggest West Indian event in New York City, the annual West Indian Day Parade.

the saint, covered with dollar bills, is paraded up and down Mulberry Street, and Italian cooking and operatic music struggle to give an authentic air to an event whose very success threatens to turn it into a fast-food tourist jamboree.

CULTURE FEST

Festivals of a different kind, mainly concentrated in summer and early autumn, bear witness to New York's superabundant cultural life. The New York Jazz Festival, the Film Festival and the multi-media Lincoln Centre Festival are among the most prestigious items in a stunning programme that takes in all the arts. But perhaps the most extraordinary feature of this festival season is the number of free events, mounted in a city reputedly dedicated to the pursuit of the Almighty Dollar. Lincoln Centre follows its July festival with high-quality dance and theatrical performances, open to all as part of its Out-of-Doors Festival in August. The New York Philharmonic and Metropolitan Opera give concerts in the parks, and in Central Park the Delacorte Theatre puts on its Shakespeare-in-the-Park performances.

Celebration of national holidays is not always notably exuberant. Perhaps as a tribute to the summer heat, New Yorkers tend to observe Independence Day on 4 July without too much expenditure of effort, by watching spectacular firework displays, especially down on the East River waterfront. The weather has cooled – or worse – by the last day of October, when citizens celebrate Hallowe'en by decorating their homes with pumpkins and spooky accessories, and a procession of figures in fantastic costumes winds its way through Greenwich Village in an annual display of grotesquerie. In a nicely judged juxtaposition, the New York Marathon – the greatest mass movement of its kind – is scheduled to take place a day or two before or after the night when the devils, witches and bohemians come out on parade.

In chilly November, on Veterans' Day (formerly Armistice Day, 11 November), the survivors of America's wars parade down Fifth Avenue and revive memories of past glories and sacrifices. Thanksgiving Day comes round again shortly afterwards, beginning the countdown to the festive season and another impossibly crowded calendar of events.

ABOVE Food stalls (top) and exotic floats at the spectacular National Puerto Rican Day Parade.

SAN GENNARO

OOD & DR

A lunch counter in the 1950s. With its concentration of rapid transit commuters moving to and from their places of work with little time to spare, the food-on-the-move ethic has long been part of New York eating culture.

New Yorkers are as different from each other as they are from other Americans. Many are recent arrivals – one in three is foreign born – and their city is noisier, more densely populated and older than virtually any other American city. New York also tends to attract people who demand excellence of themselves and who expect it of others – especially in food, and often in loud voices. 'Excuse me!' Waves of migration have created their own ethnic neighbourhoods, each with its distinct cuisine and cooking smells. These areas in turn have lives of their own, swelling at certain times, then often fading and shrinking as succeeding generations move away.

PIZZA AND PASTA

Perhaps the most obvious ethnic influence on New York eating is the pizza; the poor people's food from Naples is now available at practically every subway exit in the City. 'Gimme a slice' is the basic order: crust, tomato sauce and melted cheese. This can be covered in garlic powder, crushed red pepper or Italian herbs at no extra cost. Extras, such as pepperoni, mushrooms and sausage proliferate in white plastic lettered lists. Apart from the well-known round-shaped pizza, the Sicilian is another of the great sellers – this time it's rectangular and surrounded with a thick crust. Other recipes have taken on delicious lives of their own – no longer recognisable in Italy – but oft repeated in New York.

At the other end of the Italian scale is Le Cirque's Sirio Macioni's Pasta Primavera, which apparently became so popular he removed it from the menu because he was afraid the restaurant was becoming a one-dish establishment. He has, however, generously revealed the recipe to cookbook authors so others can repeat the treat at home.

Little Italy itself is a popular tourist destination where the restaurants along Mulberry Street are practically all that remain of a neighbourhood which in the second half of the 19th century stretched from Houston

ABOVE LEFT All part of the ritual – a pizza cook flipping dough in the air.

ABOVE A typical trattoria restaurant in Little Italy.

BELOW Like most foods in New York, Italian fare is as often bought on the street as in restaurants or delis.

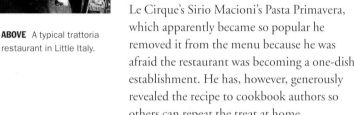

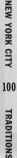
ABOVE A cake and pastry stall at the September street festival (St Gennaro) in Little Italy.

BELOW A sausage and salami stall at the same annual event.

Street to Canal Street and from the Bowery to Broadway. Many of these are the enormously popular and lively 'family-style' restaurants where vast quantities of food are served not in individual portions, but to the entire table. Home-style, original meat sauces pay little attention to waistline obsessions elsewhere in the city. Little Italy also hosts the Italian festival in the summer – the San Gennaro streetfair – the food lovers' paradise.

Neighbouring Chinatown has meantime exploded, in all its noisy and colourful glory, outwards to the north and east: noise, no English, squirming live fish, glistening roast duck and sausages. Recent immigration from the People's Republic of China and Hong Kong has swelled the population immensely and with it the range of foods available – including products from Thailand and Vietnam. Chinatown's Dim Sum brunch in many of the eateries is always hugely popular. Smaller hubs in Brooklyn's Sunset Park and Queens' Flushing also support an exciting array of several Asian cuisines.

Because of NY's position as a port different kinds of seafood came early on to dominate daily menus. Lobsters and oysters were particularly abundant. Much of the seafood destined for other American markets

ARLECCHINO
RISTORANTE ITALIANO

192 BLEECKER STREET
NEW YORK, N.Y. 10012
212-475-2355

ABOVE Street shopping for vegetables is nowhere more entertaining than in New York's Chinatown.

passes through Fulton market, as do many restaurateurs early in the morning in order to bargain for the freshest seafood. The surrounding South Street Seaport – very close to Wall Street – has developed into a thriving area full of shops, restaurants and the varied antics of outdoor street performers. The Grand Central Oyster Bar in Grand Central Station is one of many places continuing to pay tribute to this tradition, having been through several incarnations since it first opened in 1913. Its cavernous ceilings make a din out of lunch conversation, but the atmosphere more than compensates.

Manhattan Clam Chowder is all about tomatoes. The New England version of this venerable soup, which was originally made by fishermen themselves, includes bacon, onion, potatoes, crackers and clams. Such was the horror of those living further north at non-traditional (red-tinged) recipes that a Maine legislator in 1939 introduced a bill outlawing the use of tomatoes in chowder. Eventually the fuss died down and in Manhattan the tomatoes have stayed.

Spanish is definitely the second language of New York. Hispanic people from all over Latin America have flocked to the city with Puerto Ricans making up one of the largest groups. Puerto Rican food is a combination of the influences of the indigenous taino Indians, African slaves and the Spanish. The

CHINESE
at BERNSTEIN'S on Essex

AUTHENTIC CHINESE CUI

Under Supervision of Rabbi J.H. R

KOSHER
CHINESE

ABOVE Customers at Sylvia's, the Harlem soul food restaurant on Lenox Avenue between 126th and 127th Streets.

LEFT Two customers enjoy Chinese cuisine prepared by Chinese chefs to strictly kosher guidelines in a New York kosher restaurant's 'Chinese Night'.

BELOW Starbucks, a chain of NY coffee shops which has been one of the fastest-growing fast-food outlets of recent years.

staple beans rice with fried plantains is a must. But try Aroz con Pollo, pigeon peas and flan as well. Cuban Chinese is another idiosyncratic New York cuisine.

Many of the diner-style coffee shops throughout the city are run by Greeks and provide an easily affordable source of standard items like spinach pie, Greek salad or regular diner fare. But the restaurants of Astoria in Queens – Little Athens – basically cater for the city's Greek population so their hearty food is exuberantly authentic.

Brooklyn's Atlantic Avenue between Henry and Clinton Streets is the heart of the Arab community, the wonderful provisions store The Shahadi Importing Company being the longest running shop on the block.

Soul food is another city speciality. Sylvia's on Harlem Lenox Avenue and the Pink Teacup in the West Village used to be the flagships but these days have plenty more company in other neighbourhoods.

African restaurants also continue to expand in numbers, especially in the Bronx and Harlem, including a grouping around the Malcolm Shabbaz mosque.

In the West Indian and Caribbean neighbourhood of Crown Heights the cooking is of island flavours.

KOSHER PARADISE

New York is noticeably a Jewish city and a large number of the foods associated with American Jews have again become fashionable: knishes and blintzes for a start.

Katz's survives on the lower East side. An original Jewish deli of the old kind, bustling as ever (although its original neighbourhood has gone) with a huge communal dining room. A pastrami sandwich (Yiddish for seasoned smoked beef) is what you should order here – a small mountain of succulent beef slices on rye with sour pickles on the side – and forget about calorie and cholesterol counts. With luck you might get the table where Meg Ryan had such a good time in *When Harry Met Sally*. 'Hope you have what she had. Enjoy!' says the hand-written sign on the napkin dispenser. To drink? Maybe a Cel-Ray soda or an egg cream.

The egg cream is another quirky New York special. The very mention of the name brings forth smiles and stories of nostalgia for the soda fountains of yore. This fizzy froth, somewhat surprisingly, is made of milk, soda and chocolate syrup. No one seems to know what happened to the egg or the cream.

Two other New York drinks to taste are the chocolate Yoo Hoo and the coffee-flavoured Manhattan Special.

Bagels were another item enjoyed within the city's largest Eastern European Jewish community. The recipe was a closely guarded secret passed down the generations within baker families. Nowadays machines handle all stages of the process but purists say the bread circle should be formed by hand rather than extruded like doughnuts, which they say makes the dough tough. The formed dough is then boiled before baking to produce the classic chewy centre and superb crisp outside.

Plain bagels are all that true fans want but poppy seed, sesame seed, cinnamon, garlic and blueberry all exist. (You know you are in a multi-ethnic city when green-coloured bagels are sold on St Patrick's day!)

LEFT The ever-popular Katz's Deli on the corner of Houston and Ludlow Street.

BELOW Mama's Kosher Dairy – and deli – on the lower East Side.

BOTTOM Hot bagels are another take-away favourite in New York. This shop is on Flatbush Avenue, Brooklyn.

ABOVE The interior of the Jezebel Restaurant in the heart of New York's Theatre District.

RIGHT The world famous Zabar's Delicatessen on the upper West Side.

BELOW One of the most fashionable eating places in the City, the River Cafe is situated in Brooklyn with a stunning view of the Manhattan skyline.

A lesser known but equally quintessential part of the New York experience is lox – brine-cured and lightly smoked salmon – another Eastern European tradition. Estimates vary as to the figures for smoked fish sold annually in New York but it is certainly more than anywhere else in the world. The food store Zabar's alone sold 4,545 kilograms (10,000 pounds) of smoked salmon over the 97/98 holiday period.

Cream cheese is a major ingredient in cheesecake, another dish associated with New York City – variously attributed to Italian or Jewish culinary traditions – and many variations survive. Juniors of Brooklyn advertise on a large billboard beside the Brooklyn–Queens Expressway in an otherwise extremely dreary part of town that they make the best cheesecake in the world. Maybe they do. It's hard to choose between pineapple and strawberry topping – perhaps better to take the traditional daunting plain. Certainly there always seems to be a line of cars double-parked outside – testament to something.

DINNERS AND DINERS

Automats, the self-service restaurants which flourished in New York during the 20s, 30s and 40s were actually operated by a Philadelphia company, Horn and Hardart. The first automat opened in Times Square in 1912. The items sold all cost five cents – a nickel – behind glass doors which opened with a coin in a slot. The coffee was widely held to be New York's best. During the 1930s lunch and dinner became available. Sadly for folklore fast-food operations saw the automats out. The last one closed in 1991.

Some of the best restaurants are household names the world over. The Union Square Café, is a consistent favourite, The Gotham Bar & Grill, the Café des Artistes, Le Cirque, The Four Seasons, One If By Land and Peter Luger appear again and again on reviewers' lists and the lips of would-be diners.

CAFE DES ARTISTES

The River Café

Brunch

Do not despair of ever being able to afford
to eat dinner in any of them – many have a
far more affordable *prix fixe* lunch and every
summer many restaurants participate in
New York Restaurant Week during which
the price of lunch corresponds to the current
year. Under this system, in the year 2000
lunch costs $20.00 Needless to say,
reservations fill quickly.

New Yorkers tend to rely somewhat on a
slim volume called the *Zagat New York City
Restaurant Guide*, which is widely available
and in 1998 listed nearly 2,000 restaurants
(although there are probably somewhere near
15,000 overall). *Zagat's* contains the views
of New York's own – over 17,000 people
participate in their surveys, eating over three
million restaurant meals in the process.

For the crowd that wants to stay up all
night New York has much on offer. A classic
is the Empire Diner in Chelsea's 10th Avenue
at 22nd Street. It never closes, has live music
during the small hours and is a great place to
breakfast: one of the few authentic example
of 'ye olde' diners in the city.

Location plays a prominent part in several
other well-known New York establishments.
What better place could there be to take
afternoon tea than at Windows on the World,
107 floors up in the World Trade Centre
building with its dizzying views out over the
harbour and surrounding boroughs? Only

slightly more down to earth at the 65th floor is the Rainbow Room at the Rockefeller Centre. Countless dreams and romances have been launched from this platform and for those who can't possibly afford dinner here, a drink at the bar is always a possibility. Similarly, many other of New York's smartest restaurants and hotels have bars where it is possible to go to enjoy the view – out the window or of the other guests – with no obligation to dine.

BARS'N'STARS

The Tavern on the Green which is inside Central Park with its exuberant foliage animals outside is where all participants in the New York Marathon go for their ritual night-before-the-race pasta dinner. A walk or roller blade through the park before or after your meal adds yet another diversion.

One relic of Irish migration to the city are the Irish bars amongst the thousands of other drinking places in the city. Probably the most famous of these is McSorley's Old Alehouse, which has been in the same Greenwich Village location since 1854. It gained a brief notoriety in the early 70s when, after over a century of being 'men only', it was taken to court – successfully – by women's groups, thereby establishing a multi-sex regime. It remains today a genuine 'sawdust' saloon, serving good beers and bar-style lunches.

LEFT The Empire Diner in all its Art Deco glory.

BELOW The trademark of the American diner is cooks working behind the front counter while the customers eat.

The 17th century saw brewing well established as a small-scale industry in New York. Early techniques were of English origin and produced beers which did not require cooking and were drunk at room temperatures. German brewers later brought techniques requiring cooler treatment. The 'lager' they produced was naturally very popular in New York's summer heat.

Early distilling involved making rum from Caribbean sugar cane. By 1770 there were four rum distillers in Manhattan. When whiskey took over as the favoured spirit production had moved elsewhere.

During Prohibition times the sale of alcoholic beverages was forbidden by the Eighteenth Amendment in 1920. This did not necessarily mean that local private enterprise failed to flourish and in true New York style the needs of the market were met.

ABOVE Inside McSorleys, still a haven for men meeting for a drink after work – but now women can come too!

BELOW McSorleys in the 1940s, with a 'Welcome Home' sign for troops returning from the War.

Current liquor laws allow bars to stay open until 4 a.m. and most do until at least 1 or 2 a.m. New York also has restrictions on the sale of packaged liquor on Sunday. Persons under the age of 21 are prohibited from consuming alcohol and minors are not allowed in bars, not even to order non-alcoholic beverages. They are, however, usually welcomed in the dining areas of restaurants where alcohol may be served.

These days nationally made beers are widely available but most stores and bars offer local brews – some made on the premises in micro breweries or beer pubs. A wide choice of imported beers is available and Californian, New York State and other American wines are an interesting addition to imported cellars.

Several popular cocktails originated in New York City including the Bloody Mary

ABOVE The White Horse Tavern on Hudson Street is most famous for the fact that the Welsh poet Dylan Thomas drank his last there before dying that same night in 1953.

BELOW The Cedar Tavern, Chumley's and Fanelli's are all bars frequented in the past by New York's artists and writers.

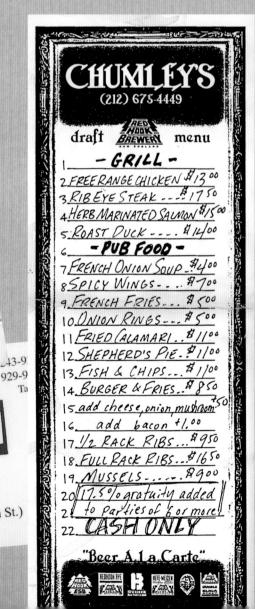

FANELLI'S CAFE
SINCE 1872
94 PRINCE ST.
NEW YORK, NY 10012
212-226-9412
FOR SAFETY • STRIKE ON BACK

212 / 741-9754
Roof Garden

CEDAR
Tavern & Roof Garden

82 University Place (Bet. 11th & 12th St.)
New York, N.Y. 10003

CHUMLEY'S
(212) 675-4449

draft RED HOOK BREWERY menu

- GRILL -
2 FREE RANGE CHICKEN $13.00
3 RIB EYE STEAK $17.50
4 HERB MARINATED SALMON $15.00
5 ROAST DUCK $14.00

- PUB FOOD -
7 FRENCH ONION SOUP $4.00
8 SPICY WINGS.... $7.00
9 FRENCH FRIES.... $5.00
10 ONION RINGS--- $5.00
11 FRIED CALAMARI.. $11.00
12 SHEPHERD'S PIE. $11.00
13 FISH & CHIPS... $11.00
14 BURGER & FRIES. $8.50
15 add cheese, onion, mushroom .50
16 add bacon +1.00
17 1/2 RACK RIBS... $9.50
18 FULL RACK RIBS... $16.50
19 MUSSELS...... $9.00
20 17.5% gratuity added
21 to parties of 6 or more
22 **CASH ONLY**

"Beer A La Carte"

(vodka and tomato juice), first served at the
St Regis Hotel; the Bronx (gin, vermouth and
orange juice), which was launched at the
Waldorf Hotel (home of the Waldorf Salad)
in 1906; and the Manhattan (bourbon and
sweet vermouth), which is thought to have
been invented before 1900 by a bartender at
the Manhattan Club.

One good place to eat in any city is where
the artists are. Soho (south of Houston Street)
in lower Manhattan was gradually penetrated
by artists in search of low rents in the 1960s
and 70s. In 1973 the New York City
Landmarks Commission designated Soho a
Historic District because of its architecture.
All this left in its wake a busy and buzzing
centre of fashionable boutiques, galleries and
bars but the pioneers themselves have for the
most part been forced out by terrific rent
rises. Tribeca, the area to the south of Canal
Street, is another area for serious restaurant
dining. Many stars have opened restaurants in
this area: Robert De Niro's, called TriBeCa
and located in Hell's kitchen, is always busy.

Artists and others have now moved to
Williamsburg, previously a rather dreary
neighbourhood across the East River, which
in 1903 the Williamsburg Bridge made
accessible to the masses in the overpopulated
Lower East Side. In Williamsburg the modest
brick-fronted buildings and smaller wooden

BELOW A famous East
Village hang-out, the
St Mark's Bar and Grill.

112

TRADITIONS

houses on side streets are being renovated and used as studios. The neighbourhood used to be Polish, like nearby Greenpoint, which still remains heavily so. There are also strict Jewish neighbourhoods close by.

CONEY AND QUEENS

For Indian food, Jackson Heights in Queens is definitely the place to go. The 74th Street section of Jackson Heights at 35th Avenue is at most times of the day just busy, busy, busy. The small-scale buildings are not that much different from those in other parts of the borough of Queens, but they have been transformed by both the contents and the customers. Brightly coloured fabrics and travel posters for Asian destinations meld with the varied blend of shoppers who are likely to have come originally from India, Pakistan or Bangladesh. Saris and sneakers are both equally at home.

COCKTAILS

NATHAN'S

The Jackson Heights Diner is one of several restaurants which serves simple, delicious and generous buffet-style food. Aisha Spices and Patel Brothers are both great places to stock up on ingredients to take home. For those who don't want to leave Manhattan there are clusters of Indian restaurants on Lexington Avenue between 27th and 28th Streets and on 6th Street between First and Second Avenues.

Take the subway to Coney Island any Saturday evening in summer and you'll be transported to yet another country – Russia. Get off at Brighton Beach stop and walk towards the sea and on to the boardwalk and you hit Odessa – well at least you're among one of the city's strongest recent migrations, from the Black Sea location. Very little English is spoken here, extensive gold jewellery is worn, fashions and hairstyles are slightly dated and many strollers do not diet – a testament to the fine local kitchens.

Coney Island is also home to another New York classic – the hot dog. An original store, Nathan's Famous, still stands near the boardwalk at the corner of Surf Avenue, along with the remnants of all the other side shows that once made Coney Island a glittering fantasy land. This stand alone sells over a million hot dogs a year – a basic frankfurter in a roll with mustard, onion and sauerkraut if you want it. Can nostalgia taste that good?

STREET CUISINE

Throughout Manhattan are the city's 4,000 licensed street vendors. Kosher frankfurters, falafel, baked potatoes, tamales, tacos, chestnuts and honey-roasted almonds are among their offerings. Look for a queue: successful vendors tend to ply their trade in the same spot for years and the locals know. Even the simplest rock salt-encrusted pretzel and a bottle of water can be a sustaining treat during a day's sight-seeing.

Some carts no doubt leave little to be desired on the housekeeping front and sell distinctly disappointing fare but they are a minority. The south side of Canal Street, between Lafayette and Mulberry Streets is always a hive of activity, but there are many other popular clusters throughout the city.

Many neighbourhoods are still blessed with old-fashioned grocery shops which are still well patronised. The ubiquitous Korean-

ABOVE A merchant dips into vats of pickled vegetables for a customer on Essex Street, on the lower East Side.

OPPOSITE Then and now; Nathan's Famous Hot Dog Emporium in Coney Island in 1954 (top) and today.

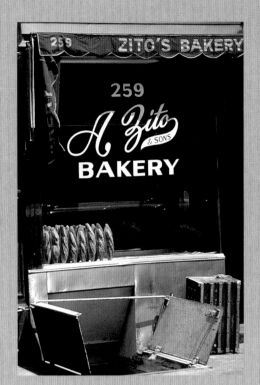

ABOVE An institution: Zito's Bakery on Bleecker Street, Greenwich Village.

OPPOSITE A street vendor setting up his pretzel stand in New York, late 1940s.

run stores all seem to present their quality fruit and vegetables in exactly the same way as though there is a school somewhere where assistants learn this exact style. Korean stores also often offer salad bars which include not only vegetable dishes but also substantial meat and pasta dishes for take-home consumption, all sold by weight.

Many fruits and vegetables, which for a long time were sold only in certain areas, have become widely available essentials: fresh basil, arugula (rocket) and cilantro (coriander) spring to mind along with broccoli rabe, mangoes, fresh lychees, clementines, lemongrass and live toads.

The city-sponsored green markets held on different days throughout New York City have been an important part of the wave to provide fresh ingredients. Specialist farmers from upstate truck in their grown produce – flowers, fruit and vegetables – along with cheeses, preserves, bread and other baked goods.

At the specialist end of the market, stores like Balducci's, Dean and De Luca's and Zabar's are a sensory experience enough just to cruise even if you don't buy. Balducci's is like an ever-enfolding cave with a series of alcoves offering more and more delights – fresh vegetables, fish, meats, cheeses, baked goods and preserved versions of all the above from the world over. Zabar's, too, has its own distinct atmosphere – very much of the Upper West Side. These and other similarly respected stores are regarded pretty much as cultural centres by New Yorkers and should be treated so by any visitor. Mail order can extend their treats to any part of the globe.

BALDUCCI'S

RIGHT A cook preparing pies at the famous deli Dean and De Luca's at 560 Broadway.

DE LUCA'S

MUSIC 118-

Text: Holly George-Warren

141

Many of New York's music venues have a place in the history of popular music, like Harlem's Apollo Theatre which has played host to jazz, blues, rock'n'roll and soul. Here in the early 60s it's a Motown package show.

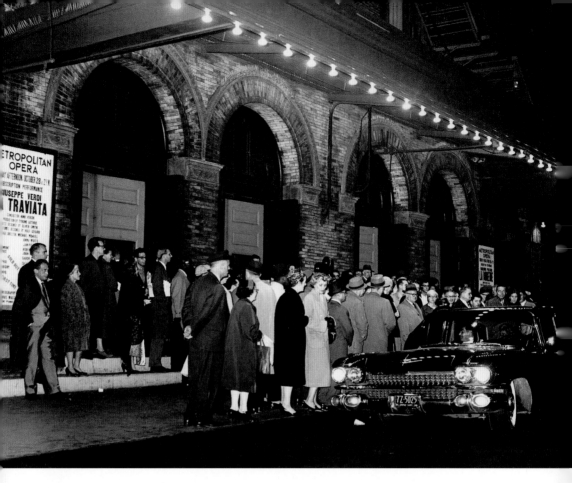

Scattered about New York City, standing before a kaleidoscope of buildings (some striking, others quite mundane) are simple black and white signposts emblazoned with the words 'New York City Music Trail'. Each describes the nightclub, concert hall or other landmark where significant musical events have taken – or now take – place. Indeed, more than a century ago, New York City became America's music mecca, with all types of musical entertainment – from high brow to low brow – presented within the walls of architecture's latest accomplishments. As times and musical tastes changed, the cutting edge could still be found in New York City – in a myriad of places. Today, as it approaches the millennium, New York City continues to pulsate with a collage of sounds thriving in a smorgasbord of venues, from architectural milestones to Bowery dives.

METROPOLITAN OPERA HOUS

For over a hundred years, New York has
been renowned for its Tin Pan Alley, and the
changing location of this pop songwriting
epicentre is symbolic of the peripatetic nature
of the city's entertainment showplaces. In the
mid-19th century, Tin Pan Alley, which got
its name from the panoply of sounds wafting
from buildings full of song publishers and
composers creating their works, existed on
East 14th Street. It's hard to believe that
today's boisterous byway was then a
fashionable boulevard and the home of the
ritzy Academy of Music (described in detail
in Edith Wharton's *Age of Innocence*), which
was built in 1854 and presented such stars as
Jenny Lind. In 1893, Tin Pan Alley relocated
to West 28th Street and Broadway, dubbed
the Great White Way, which had exploded
with fancy new theatres (notably Koster and
Bial's Concert Hall, Proctor's Music Hall and
the Grand Opera House), hosting vaudeville,
light opera and other affordable entertainments appealing to the masses. That same
year, the upscale Metropolitan Opera House
opened eleven blocks north on West 39th
Street. Nearby, architect Stanford White's
lavish Madison Square Garden, built in 1890,
presented a cavalcade of entertainment.

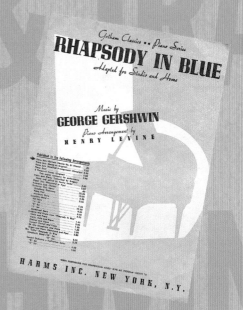

ABOVE LEFT Concertgoers
stand in line outside the
Metropolitan Opera House,
before it relocated to the
Lincoln Centre.

RIGHT George (at the
piano) and Ira Gershwin.
George Gershwin's
'Rhapsody In Blue' has
become almost a theme
tune for New York City.

ABOVE Jerry Leiber and Mike Stoller, greatest of Brill Building songsmiths.

Eventually, the Garden relocated three times, first in 1925 and most recently in 1968 to its present location atop Pennsylvania Station at Seventh Avenue and West 34th Street. Famous events held within the modern-day arena include the Concert for Bangladesh and the No Nukes Concert. In the 1990s Madison Square Garden hosts major concert tours, as well as sporting events and the Ringling Brothers Barnum and Bailey Circus. Sadly, the original Gardens were torn down decades ago.

TIN PAN ALLEY

Around the turn of the century, elaborate theatres (such as the Empire and the Olympia) presenting vaudeville, drama and comedy began crowding 42nd Street and its environs, an area previously known as Longacre Square but changed in 1904 to Times Square. Tin Pan Alley followed suit, when its song-publishing headquarters became located primarily at the Brill Building, 1619 Broadway, where it remains to this day. There, over the course of several decades, some of pop's most brilliant songwriters – including Johnny Mercer, Sammy Cahn, Neil Sedaka, Leiber and Stoller, Carole King, Cynthia Weil, Neil Diamond and Lou Reed(!), to name a few – toiled away, resulting in countless hits.

Decorative theatres with comfortable seating were not the only entertainment palaces abounding in the Times Square area. Huge dance halls, such as Roseland and the Grand Central Palace, opened in the second decade of the 20th century to capitalise on the dance craze that was sweeping the city. The April 1915 issue of *Vanity Fair* magazine pointed out, 'At last a New Yorker can look a Parisian in the face. No more need he stand by and hear ... those old familiar stories of all night life in Paris ... Now a New York man can dance until 6 a.m.' Jitterbuggers and Lindy-hoppers bopped to the beat provided by bands playing ragtime, the musical antecedent to that great American music form – jazz.

LEFT The Brill Building, hub of the American pop song business since the early 1920s

BELOW The Roseland Ballroom still continues its afternoon tea dances which started in the 20s, the venue surviving by staging rock concerts during the evenings.

BOTTOM The Times Square area at night.

RO1018 G.A. GEN ADM ADC
25.00 GEN ADM
4.25 GEN ADM
G.A. 25
CA 1X
GEN ADM
CH131F
6AUG94

BOB DYLAN

ROSELAND
239 W 52ND ST., NYC
TUE OCT 18,1994 8:00PM

HARLEM SHUFFLE

In the 1920s jazz was just beginning to blossom in New York. Its most famous home was the Cotton Club, which opened in Harlem on 142nd Street between Lenox and Fifth Avenues. From 1923 to 1935 such superstars as Duke Ellington, Cab Calloway and Josephine Baker performed at the famed hotspot. Society's elite made the trip uptown to check out the new music's most acclaimed black jazz players. (A new Cotton Club operates today at 125th Street and Broadway, and features jazz, blues and gospel.)

Another famous Harlem music landmark opened its doors right before the original Cotton Club closed. In 1934, the Apollo Theatre began presenting such legendary black artists as Bessie Smith, Billie Holiday, and Count Basie. The theatre had originally been constructed in 1913 as the Hurtig and Seaman Theatre and six years later became the New Burlesque Theatre, which – like the Cotton Club in its early years – did not allow blacks in the audience. A black impresario named Ralph Cooper took it over in 1934, changing the admission policy and featuring 'Jazz à la Carte', in which he starred with Benny Carter and an orchestra of '16 Gorgeous Steppers'. In the decades to come, the Apollo became famous for its amateur night, when new talent auditioned before discerning – and often harsh – audiences. The rafters reverberated over the years with stellar artists appearing on the Apollo stage: James Brown (1956), the Motown Revue starring Marvin Gaye, the Miracles, the Supremes, the Marvellettes, and 12-year-old Stevie Wonder (1962), and the young Jackson 5 (1969).

Legend has it that the first white act to appear at the Apollo was Buddy Holly and the Crickets in the 1950s; although upon being booked, they had been mistaken for a black act. When they turned up as white musicians, they won the crowd over with their infectious rock 'n' roll.

ABOVE Billie Holiday was one of the jazz greats who appeared at the Apollo Theatre in Harlem.

LEFT Duke Ellington and his Orchestra was the house band at the Cotton Club for a number of years.

INSET LEFT The Cotton Club in its 1930s heyday – here advertising a show by Cab Calloway.

THE APOLLO

The Apollo closed in 1975 and briefly became a movie house. In 1983 it reopened, presenting such acts as Parliament/Funkadelic and reviving its Original Amateur Night, which continues every Wednesday and is broadcast on television. Tours of the theatre are conducted daily. Starting in 1942, Apollo headliners began dropping by the nearby Showman's Café, a jazz supperclub, which moved locations in recent years to 2321 Eighth Avenue at 125th Street.

HALLOWED HALLS

A few other Manhattan theatres lay claim to the longevity enjoyed by the Apollo. The oldest and most venerable is Carnegie Hall, which was built in 1891, on the corner of 57th Street and Seventh Avenue. This hallowed hall has seen artists ranging from Enrico Caruso and Leadbelly to Buck Owens and the Buckaroos and the Beatles in their New York concert debut in 1964.

Perhaps the most unusual theatre in New York is the City Centre, on West 55th Street between Sixth and Seventh Avenues, which was originally constructed in 1924 as the Mecca Temple by members of the Ancient and Accepted Order of the Mystic Shrine. Still with its original Spanish tiled, domed facade, it became a theatre presenting music and other performing arts in the 1940s when it was saved from the wrecking ball by Mayor Fiorello LaGuardia.

Another landmark building, with a lovely baroque interior, is the Beacon Theatre, built in 1928 on Broadway and 75th Street. Shuttered for several years, today the reopened theatre presents a variety of pop, blues and rock concerts, including more intimate sets by rock legends (including Bob Dylan, Van Morrison, and Bruce Springsteen, in recent years).

New York's most fabulous historic theatre is the 1932 Art Deco masterpiece, Radio City Music Hall, located at Sixth Avenue and 50th Street. Although synonymous with the leggy Rockettes troup of dancing girls and holiday show extravaganzas, the 6,200-seat theatre has featured artists ranging from Talking Heads to Frank Sinatra and Tina Turner. Guided tours of Radio City are conducted several times daily. Within its opulent Deco interior is the city's largest Wurlitzer pipe organ.

FAR RIGHT The most famous concert venue in New York, Carnegie Hall.

RIGHT The Apollo Theatre's amateur nights were a potent launching pad for new talent.

BELOW From New Jersey, Bruce Springsteen was just one star who has played the reopened Beacon Theatre.on Broadway.

BOTTOM RIGHT The Rockettes, the dancing girls who have come to be synonymous with Radio City Music Hall.

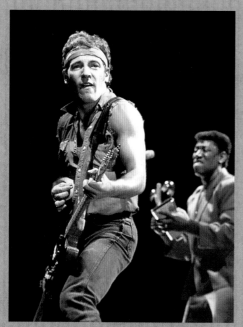

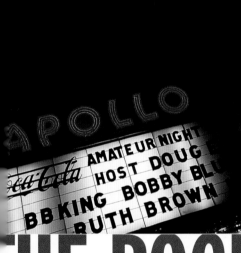

APOLLO

Coca-Cola AMATEUR NIGHT
HOST DOUG E
BB KING BOBBY BLU
RUTH BROWN

THE ROCKETTES

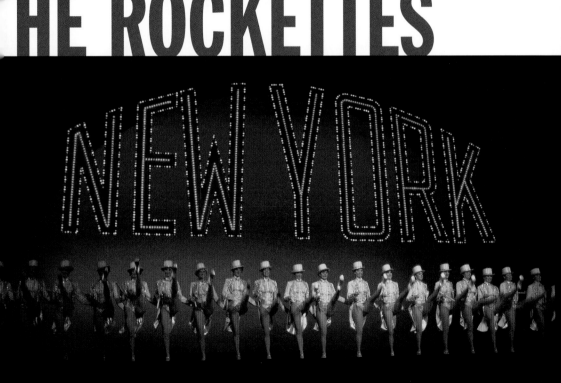

NEW YORK

NEW YORK CITY OPERA

New York State Theater, Lincoln Center

Where great art, music and theater are all one destination.

ABOVE Leonard Bernstein conducting the New York Philharmonic Orchestra during a rehearsal at the Avery Fischer Hall.

LEFT The New York City Opera is based at the New York State Theatre in the Lincoln Centre.

Right up the street from Radio City is a sign designating West 52nd Street as Swing Street, honouring the big bands and jazz geniuses playing swing and later bebop in a plethora of jazz clubs such as the famed Birdland in the 1930s and 40s. Running between Fifth and Sixth Avenues, Swing Street is chockablock with plaques honouring the artists who gigged at clubs during the era's halcyon days (and nights): Dizzy Gillespie, Coleman Hawkins, Billie Holiday, Lester Young, Sarah Vaughan, Thelonious Monk and Charlie Parker. (Incidentally, downtown, a strip of Avenue B in the East Village was named Charlie Parker Place in honour of the great sax man who resided there).

Another 20 blocks upfrom Swing Street is New York's largest music complex, the Lincoln Centre. Sprawled along Broadway, beginning at 72nd Street, this group of concert halls was constructed in the 1960s in an area where previously had stood the slums inspiring the 1957 musical, *West Side Story*. The Metropolitan Opera House relocated there, along with the newly constructed Alice Tully Hall and Avery Fisher Hall (originally Philharmonic Hall), where concerts and recitals are held. Also part of the Lincoln Centre are the New York State Theatre for opera and ballet, the Vivian Beaumont Theatre and Mitzi E. Newhouse theatre for plays, the New York Public Library for the Performing Arts , the Walter Reade Theatre and the Julliard School. On the grand plaza, there is the Damrosch bandstand where outdoor concerts presenting diverse types of music (from bluegrass to polka to salsa) are held. Jazz at the Lincoln Centre is an annual event featuring all kinds of jazz performances, including Afro-Cuban music, big-band swing and the music's latest young Turks.

ABOVE A 1997 ad from the *Village Voice* showing that Birdland is still going strong as a jazz centre.

BELOW LEFT 52nd Street in its 'Swing Street' days when it was the centre of the world of jazz.

BELOW RIGHT A group led by the legendary Charlie Parker (right) playing at Birdland in 1949.

MUSIC

129

NEW YORK CITY

ABOVE The famed Village Vanguard jazz club on Seventh Avenue in Greenwich Village.

BELOW The 'Vanguard and Sweet Basil are just two of the many jazz spots alive and kicking in the Village.

JAZZ LIVE AT THE

VILLAGE VANGUARD

★ NOW THRU SUNDAY APRIL 13TH ★

★ DAVID SANCHEZ ★
QUINTET
★ EDSEL GOMEZ - JOHN BENITEZ ★
★ ADAM CRUZ - PERNELL SATURNINO ★

★ APRIL 15TH - APRIL 20TH ★

WESSELL ANDERSON
QUINTET
★ STEFON HARRIS - ERIC LEWIS ★
★ ERIC REVIS - DANA MURRAY ★

★ APRIL 22ND - APRIL 27TH ★
CHARLES McPHERSON QUARTET

MONDAY NIGHTS **THE VANGUARD JAZZ ORCHESTRA**

Baldwin

SETS: MON THRU THURS & SUN - 9:30 & 11:30
FRI & SAT - 9:30, 11:30 & 1:00AM 255-40

178 7TH. AVE. SOUTH AT 11TH STREET

SWEET BASIL
APRIL
TUESDAY THRU SUNDAY
APRIL 8 - 13

CRAIG HANDY QUARTET
DAVID KIKOSKI, DWAYNE BURNO, GENE JACKSON

APRIL 15 - 20
JANE IRA BLOOM QUARTET
FRED HERSH, MARK DRESSER, BOBBY PREVITE

EVERY MONDAY THE MUSIC OF: **THE SPIRIT OF LIFE ENSEMBLE**

SATURDAY JAZZ BRUNCH
NO COVER 2 - 6 PM
ILHAN ERSAHIN QUARTET

THE ORIGINAL JAZZ BRUNCH
EVERY SUN. 2-6PM NO COVER
LEGENDARY TRUMPETER
DOC CHEATHAM

www.sweetbasil.com

BRUNCH • LUNCH • DINNER • LATE SUPPER
7 Days Noon 2AM CREDIT CARDS
88 SEVENTH AVE. SO. Res: 242-1785

Uptown is by no means the only section of Manhattan where a vibrant music scene has thrived. Jazz clubs began proliferating in the West Village in the 1940s and 50s. Pre-eminent among them is the Village Vanguard, which opened in the late 30s. *New York Times* jazz critic, Peter Watrous, has called it 'the standard against which all other jazz spaces are judged'. Located on West 11th Street, the acoustically superb club has booked all the greats and continues to do so. If those walls could talk!

The West Village also kicked off the folk-music craze in the late 50s/early 60s within the smoky environs of its clubs and coffee-houses. Gerdes Folk City opened at the first of its three locations in 1959 at 11 West Fourth Street. Its Monday night hootenannies saw the debuts of Bob Dylan and Simon and Garfunkel (then billed Tom and Jerry). One of Folk City's locations now houses the Bottom Line, which in its 20-plus years has presented legendary performances by about-to-break artists like Bruce Springsteen and Patti Smith. (The smoke-free club is still one of the best venues to see artists ranging from Joan Baez, who recorded a double live album there, to Jimmie Dale Gilmore.) Village legend has it that the nearby Gaslight club was where Dylan wrote 'A Hard Rain's A-Gonna Fall' in the upstairs dressing room while waiting to go onstage. In 1961, the Bitter End opened its doors with a performance by Peter, Paul and Mary. Still a thriving club on Bleecker Street, the Bitter

BELOW Gerde's Folk City on West 4th Street, where folk music fans have long flocked to hear traditional American music.

BOTTOM RIGHT Bob Dylan in the mid-60s, not long after he had sprung to fame via venues like Gerde's, and still had a house on MacDougal Street in the West Village.

BOB DYLAN

End has had its stage graced with such luminaries as Joni Mitchell, Phil Ochs and, in recent years, Tracy Chapman. Photos of the countless folk heroes who have appeared at the Bitter End cram the walls.

ROCK'N'ROLL

Rock 'n' roll also became a national phenomenon via an assortment of New York City venues. Legendary disc jockey Alan Freed held his teenage extravaganzas in the 1950s at the Brooklyn Paramount (built in 1928 and originally featuring shows by Mae West, Bing Crosby, Ginger Rogers and Rudy Valle), on Flatbush Avenue in Downtown Brooklyn, and at Times Square's Paramount Theatre (the site of teenybopper-mobbed performances by Frank Sinatra a few years earlier). Although Manhattan's Paramount no longer exists, Brooklyn's Paramount, closed in 1962, still stands as part of Long Island University; its huge Wurlitzer pipe organ, gilt statuary and plush red seats now decorate the home of the college's basketball team, and concerts are occasionally given on the organ.

The Twist dance craze was born in the early 1960s at New York's Peppermint Lounge, on West 45th Street, as celebrated by Joey Dee and the Starlighters' hit single, 'Peppermint Twist.' The Ronettes got their start at the definitive discotheque as go-go girls, and all society flocked there to make the

BELOW Maverick DJ Alan Freed, whose early 50s radio shows virtually launched the rock'n'roll phenomenon, also toured a package show at concert venues that included the Brooklyn Paramount.

scene. Two decades later, a hip club featuring live music was named the Peppermint Lounge when it opened in 1982 downtown at Fifth Avenue and 15th Street. (It closed in 1988.) Other 1960s rock 'n' roll hotspots in midtown included Steve Paul's the Scene on West 46th Street, a basement club where Tiny Tim held court and Johnny Winter, Jim Morrison and Jimi Hendrix held late-night jams. Ondine's flourished on East 59th Street from 1966 to 67 and presented the New York debut of the Doors and Buffalo Springfield. Ungano's, on West 70th Street, saw the New York City debuts of the Allman Brothers and MC5. All are now shuttered, razed or function as run-of-the-mill businesses.

Downtown, the pre-eminent rock concert hall of the late 1960s was Bill Graham's Fillmore East on Second Avenue at Sixth Street. The Allman Brothers' 1970 live

ABOVE Customers waiting to enter the Peppermint Lounge, New York home of the Twist, in 1962.

BELOW The Allman Brothers debuted at Ungano's club on West 70th Street in the late 60s.

double album was recorded there, and elaborate psychedelic light shows provided the right ambience for tripped-out audiences. In the 1980s, the legendary theatre briefly became a gay disco. Today, the structure still stands and is currently being converted into offices. Around the corner on St Mark's Place, between Second and Third Avenues, a Polish social hall called the Dom made history with performances by the Velvet Underground and Andy Warhol's Exploding Plastic Inevitable. After her departure from the band, V.U. chanteuse Nico performed in a basement cabaret at the club, where she was backed by 16-year-old Jackson Browne. The Dom later became a trendy rock club, the Electric Circus, and today, ironically, serves as a meeting place for an assortment of 12-step programmes.

Other 60s rock 'n' roll hotspots sprung up in the West Village: the Café Au Go Go on Bleecker Street was where Cream, Frank Zappa and other notables performed in the late 60s. Café Wha? saw gigs by Jimmy James (aka Jimi Hendrix) and the Blue Flames; Chas Chandler discovered Hendrix there and brought him to England, where he became a megastar. The Lovin' Spoonful and the Blues Magoos were regulars at the Night Owl, and the Salvation Club frequently presented the Chambers Brothers and early light shows. The Café Bizarre featured the Velvet Underground before the band made their move to the Dom.

Max's Kansas City opened in 1965 as a cooler-than-cool hangout for artists, Bohos,

ABOVE The most famous New York rock venue in the late 60s was undoubtedly Bill Graham's Fillmore East.

BELOW Frank Zappa, the avant garde musician and composer who appeared at the Cafe Au Go Go.

TOP RIGHT Cafe Wha? on MacDougal Street, early in 1969

BOTTOM RIGHT Andy Warhol and singer Nico in 1966 at the Action House, a discotheque in Island Park, Long Island.

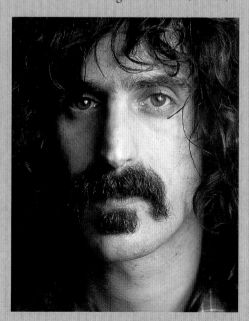

CAFE
WHA?

DEBBIE HARRY

http://www.cbgb.com

CBGB

315 BOWERY @ BLEECKER NYC (212) 982-4052

WEDNESDAY APRIL 9 · 8pm · $8
Daddy Long Head · Gnomes of Zurich
Iron Boss · Sweet Diesel
KISS IT GOODBYE · UNSANE

THURSDAY APRIL 10 · 7pm · $7
Squirrels From Hell · Eric Hamilton · Idlewilds
Pbbbst · Lucid · Isabelle's Gift
Uncle · Room On Fire

FRIDAY APRIL 11 · 9pm · $9
God Rays · Two Dollar Guitar
SLEEPYHEAD · ANTIETAM · Exactones

SATURDAY APRIL 12 · 8pm · $9
Porcelain Fish Bowl · Felix Frump
Axe to Grind · Squatweiler (Greensboro, N.C.)
Thorazine (Philadelphia) · **WIVES** · Slickpelt

SUNDAY APRIL 13 · 3pm · $6
KINGSIZE PRESENTS
Ignata · 151 · Arm (Minneapolis)
Freedom Fights · CRUTCH (Am-Rep)

SUN. & MON. EVENINGS AUDITION SHOWCASE

TUESDAY APRIL 15 · 7pm · $5
Badwrench · Wad · Paradoxical Popsicle
15 Minutes · Death Penis · Race
Rancid Pole Cats

WEDNESDAY APRIL 16 · 7pm · $5
Hidden Persuaders · Speaker · Singleman
Party · Bedpan · Cross The Line · Foma
Skingame · Gould

COMING: 4/18 Cows/Kepone
4/19 Funkface/Lordz of Brooklyn
4/20 Brutal Truth/Grief
4/21 & 4/22 Business/Madball
4/25 Spacehog
4/28 Stillsuit/Ink & Dagger

HARRY

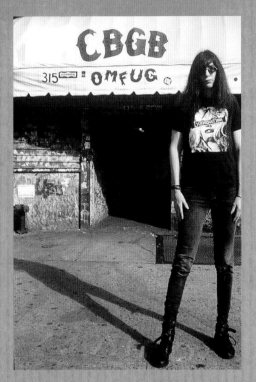

and Andy Warhol's in-crowd. Lou Reed immortalised its back room in 'Walk on the Wild Side,' and a young Debbie Harry worked as a waitress there. The club's first rock 'n' roll happening was a 1967 Beatles press conference conducted by the band's manager, Brian Epstein. In the 1970s, an upstairs space began presenting rock shows, including legendary stands by Big Star, Gram Parsons and the Fallen Angels, Iggy Pop, the latterday Velvet Underground and Bruce Springsteen. Aerosmith made its 1972 New York debut at the club. After being closed for a while in the mid-70s, Max's reopened as a punk club, featuring Johnny Thunders' Heartbreakers, Sid Vicious and other edgy performers. Woefully, the building now houses a deli; a new Max's Kansas City, presenting an homage to the original, opened amid much controversy in midtown on West 52nd Street in late 1997.

It was a Bowery dive called CBGB-OMFUG that truly gave birth to America's punk scene. Veteran music *aficionado* Hilly Kristal opened the former derelict bar called the Palace in December 1973. Kristal had previously managed the Village Vanguard in the late 50s/early 60s and had put on concerts at Central Park's Wolman Rink in the mid-60s. Originally, Kristal intended to book acoustic country, bluegrass and blues acts (thus the initials OMFUG, which stand for Other Music For Uplifting Gourmandisers). In early 1974, Kristal was convinced by Television's manager to book the fledgling band on Sunday nights, a residency that lasted for four months. Soon the Ramones, Patti Smith Group, Talking Heads and

LEFT Debbie Harry singing with Blondie onstage at CBGB in 1978.

ABOVE Joey Ramone of the Ramones in front of CBGB on the Bowery, in 1993.

LEFT BOTTOM The crowd at CBGB in 1979.

BELOW RIGHT At the reopened Max's Kansas City, the doomed Sid Vicious and Nancy Spungen.

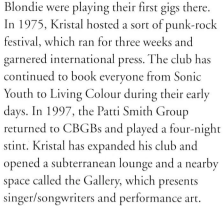

TOP Owner Steve Rubell monitoring the guest line outside Studio 54 in 1978.

ABOVE Some of the disco dancers playing ball at Studio 54 in 1981.

BELOW Punk pioneers Richard Hell and the Voidoids who played early gigs at Hurrah's.

RIGHT Disco diva Grace Jones preparing for a live appearance at Studio 54 in December 1977.

Blondie were playing their first gigs there. In 1975, Kristal hosted a sort of punk-rock festival, which ran for three weeks and garnered international press. The club has continued to book everyone from Sonic Youth to Living Colour during their early days. In 1997, the Patti Smith Group returned to CBGBs and played a four-night stint. Kristal has expanded his club and opened a subterranean lounge and a nearby space called the Gallery, which presents singer/songwriters and performance art.

While punk remained an underground scene in the 70s, disco, of course, was huge. Its most famous palace from 1977 to 1981, Studio 54 was located at (where else?) 54 West 54th Street. The hoi polloi danced beneath a giant coke spoon and moon hanging from the ceiling while Warhol and pals like Liza Minnelli, Halston and Truman Capote hobnobbed in tucked-away VIP areas. Although the music was mainly canned, occasionally bands would play; Blondie performed there when its disco crossover hit 'Heart of Glass' was feted by the club. After Studio 54's owners Steve Rubell and Ian Schrager were busted for tax evasion among other charges, the club limped along, for a while as a rock club, before shutting down. In the early 1990s, the downtown rock club, the Ritz, moved briefly into the space, and in 1997 it was used as a soundstage for a film about Studio's glory days.

Thanks to Studio 54, a sort of hybrid hipster/punk/disco club scene emerged in New York in the late 70s. Hurrahs was a spacious (by punk standards) dance club on West 69th Street, which featured early US performances by the Cure, Lene Lovich and other British bands, as well as New York stalwarts like Richard Hell and the Voidoids. The Mudd Club, with its red velvet ropes out front on Tribeca's desolate White Street, took off on Studio's snob appeal and debauched atmosphere but with a punk-rock, black leather 'n' chains aesthetic. Early gigs there included those by R.E.M. and the Go-Gos; the club ran from 1979 to 1983. A cool, hip little joint nearby, TR-3, frequently featured visiting British bands, the Slits, New Order and Delta 5. As the music's appeal evolved from underground to the masses in the 1980s, cavernous clubs opened to accommodate the mobs. The Palladium

STUDIO 54

MUDD CLUB

THE GO-GOs

(formerly a theatre that presented punk bands like the Clash, the Pretenders and PiL in the early 80s), was located at the site of the old Academy of Music on East 14th Street and was decorated by Downtown artists Kenny Scharf and Keith Haring.

Danceteria on West 37th Street gave Madonna her start when its top DJ played her demo tape; she performed on the club's roof with a backing tape soon after. Other clubs that saw lots of 80s action were in the East Village: the Ritz on East 11th Street, the World on East Second Street and the Pyramid Club on Avenue A. Featuring the occasional avant-punk act, but primarily presenting the best country (Merle Haggard), blues (John Lee Hooker), pioneering rock 'n' roll (Carl Perkins) and R 'n' B (James Brown) artists was the Lone Star, a Texas-inspired honky-tonk on Fifth Avenue at 13th Street. Sadly, of all those mentioned above, only the Pyramid (where drag queens RuPaul, Lipsynka and Lady Bunny got their starts) still exists. Today's best new clubs include S.O.B.'s (Varick Street) for Caribbean music, the Fez (Lafayette Street) for singer/songwriters, the Knitting Factory (near the old Mudd Club in Tribeca) and the Mercury Lounge (Houston Street) for cutting-edge artists, and for roots musics (New Orleans, blues, and country) Tramps on 21st Street (in the 80s, a tiny venue a few blocks east that provided homes for Big Joe Williams and Buster Poindexter).

Undeniably, New York City will continue to be one of America's hottest music capitals – not only because so much groundbreaking music and landmark entertainment has taken place in the city, but because it will undoubtedly be the creative birthplace for talent of the future.

LEFT The Go-Gos made early appearances at New York's Mudd Club.

BELOW A very early shot of Madonna, around the time the DJ played her tape at Danceteria and she sang on the roof soon after.

Text: Patrick Carroll

Baseball above all other sports has gripped the people of New York for generations. Shea Stadium, home of the Mets, is seen here filled to capacity for the fourth game of the 1969 World Series – which the Mets won.

& LEISURE
142-163

Even by American standards New Yorkers are and always have been sports mad. When the New York Yankees won the 1996 World Series, city officials estimated that three million people lined Broadway for the parade honouring the team. Allowing for some Mayor Guiliani-generated hyping of the numbers, there were a lot of people out cheering the champions; and every age group as well as social, ethnic and economic strand of the city was represented. The New York Metropolitan Area supports nine major professional sports franchises: the baseball Yankees and Mets; the football Giants and Jets; the Rangers, Islanders and New Jersey Devils of the National Hockey League; and the Knicks and New Jersey Nets of the National Basketball Association. New York's newspapers devote more space to sports reportage than to any other single subject. In addition to saturation television coverage, the city also has a 24-hour sports radio station. At a conservative estimate, one in five leisure conversations in New York City will touch on sports.

THE SPORTI

THE SPORTING ELEMENT

The southern tip of Manhattan is one of the most intensively built-up pieces of real estate in the world, but almost since Europeans arrived to stay in 1624 there has always been an open space called Bowling Green. The Dutch and English who colonised New York brought their pastimes with them and as the rigours of settler life eased they pursued them energetically. Hunting and fishing – initially needed for survival – became in time more recreational. The Dutch were skaters as well as skittlers, and the English brought with them the family of bat, ball and running games, which in time evolved into baseball. The first recognisable form of modern baseball, as codified in 1845 by members of the Knickerbocker Club, was known as 'The New York Game'.

As well as organised and semi-organised games, New York – certainly from the post-Revolutionary War period – always had a section of society that corresponded to what, in England, the Regency period author Pierce Egan described as 'The Fancy'; and which old-time New Yorkers called 'The Sporting Element'. These were the supporters and patrons particularly of prize fighting and horseracing but also of such *demi-monde*

ABOVE The New York Jets football team playing at the Meadowlands, New Jersey.

LEFT Coney Island beach was a huge attraction for the majority of New Yorkers in the 20s and 30s.

BELOW Skating in Central Park has been a popular pastime since the Park was opened, as seen in this painting from 1865.

ABOVE The Hudson and East River even provide some fishing in certain choice locations.

BELOW Outdoor sports of a very relaxed variety – men playing chess.

'sporting' activities as cock- and dog-fighting, and all forms of gambling.

In the years before and after the American Civil War, while the City was expanding rapidly, both upwards and outwards, the New York State Legislature enacted some of the most draconian anti-gambling laws in America. Despite this, by 1880 the City was estimated to have at least 200 gambling houses, and more than 2,500 people were known to the police as professional gamblers, policy dealers and lottery agents. A number of the gambling establishments were discreet and luxurious, featuring liveried servants offering fine food. The play – mainly faro and roulette – was generally fair, and the clientele respectable and even prominent; often including the same politicians who had passed the anti-gambling laws. The most famous proprietor of the higher type of New York gambling house was Richard A. Canfield (1855–1914), also a notable art collector, who had a reputation for straight dealing, and adapted for gambling the form of solitaire, or patience, which bears his mane. The lesser houses, or 'gambling heels' as they were popularly known, offered the customer no chance at all. The sucker (usually an out-of-towner) could consider himself lucky if he escaped having lost nothing more than his money.

Studies of Richard Canfield

ABOVE A New York newspaper caricature of gambling proprietor Richard Canfield.

Through much of the 1880s gaming and gamblers in New York were found mainly around lower Broadway and the Bowery, but with the new century the sporting element, along with the theatrical and nightlife worlds, moved steadily uptown, centring finally in the Times Square district: the habitat of Damon Runyon's Broadway characters and the *Telephone Booth Indians* chronicled by A.J. Leibling. Aside from the great performing athletes of the period – Babe Ruth, Jack Dempsey and Red Grange, to name only three – among the salient heroes of the pre-depression New York sporting element were George 'Tex' Rickard and Arnold Rothstein. The latter appears, heavily fictionalised, as Armand 'The Brain' Rosenthal in several Runyon stories and is described as 'well known to one and all in this town as a very large operator in gambling, and in one thing and another...'; the 'one thing and another' being basically New York's criminal underworld, of which Rothstein was an acknowledged kingpin. The coup for which Rothstein was most (in)famous involved his fixing of the 1919 World Series, whereby eight members of the Chicago White Sox allegedly took bribes to throw the Series games against Cincinnati.

The colourful Rickard (1871–1929), was a more legitimate operator. After early careers as a cowboy, gold prospector and saloon-keeper, Rickard became America's premier boxing promoter. Having organised his first world championship fight in 1906, Rickard, in 1921, promoted the first bout to gross over one million dollars (Dempsey *vs* Carpentier across the Hudson River in Jersey City). Rickard was also instrumental in the campaign to have professional boxing legalised in New York. Until it was repealed in 1920 boxing in the City was governed by the Frawley Law, which banned any but 'exhibition' bouts held in private clubs. No points decisions were allowed in these cases, only a knockout giving a clear result.

If Rickard and Rothstein can be reckoned among the patron saints of the City's sporting element then its cathedrals have been the four incarnations of Madison Square Garden. Probably the most famous indoor sports arena in the world, The Garden, as New Yorkers invariably call it, started as a disused railway depot near Madison Square Park above 23rd Street, where Broadway crosses Fifth Avenue. In the early 1870s an Irish cornet player organised band concerts on the site and it was known as 'Gilmore's Gardens'. Later the building was leased by P.T. Barnum who used it to present his many and varied attractions and promotions. The original Garden was razed in 1890 and a new one built to the design of the famous New York

ABOVE Wheeler-dealer and general fixer Arnold Rothstein who did much to established organised sport in the City.

LEFT Tex Rickard, the boxing promoter who founded Madison Square Garden as a fight venue.

BELOW A crowded Madison Square Garden on the night of the very first Golden Gloves boxing tournament in 1937.

TEX RICKARD

architect Stanford White. This elaborate building, which was topped with a larger-than-life classical statue, was a recognised New York landmark. In 1906 White was shot to death in its roof garden restaurant by a man who believed that his wife was having an affair with an architect.

In 1925 White's building was torn down and, under Rickard's supervision, a third Madison Square Garden was built on Eighth Avenue between 49th and 50th Streets. Although the fourth and present Madison Square Garden – built above Penn Station – opened in 1968, to many New Yorkers the Eighth Avenue building was the 'real' garden. In addition to its famous boxing cards it also presented ice hockey, six-day bicycle racing, basketball, athletics, tennis and wrestling. Regular extra-sporting attractions were the visits of Ringling Brothers, Barnum and Bailey's Circus, Rodeo, Horse and Dog Shows and political conventions.

The Garden, before the days of corporate hospitality suites and extortionate ticket prices, was always a curiously democratic place; the only measure of caste being money. Everyone – the Governor; the Broadway star or the wolf of Wall Street sitting at ring-, court- or rink-side; the Queen's cabbie in the mezzanine, or the same ticket scalpers who congregated in the Eighth Avenue lobby – breathed in the same Garden smell of cigar smoke, beer, hot dogs, candy floss and sweat. And everyone saw the same performance. Even if they were furthest from the action at The Garden – as at the ballpark – no one watched the game more closely than the kids, because they had to not only appreciate their heroes' performances but also needed to analyse and memorise them for imitation in the playground and on the streets.

TOP LEFT The original Madison Square Graden in an 1890 engraving.

BOTTOM LEFT The present-day Garden during an ice hockey World Cup game.

RIGHT Not as big as in Canada, but popular all the same – here the New York Rangers ice hockey team play the Calgary Flames.

SPALDEEN CITY

The spaldeen was an essential piece of sports equipment for several generations of New York City school kids. Manufactured by the firm of A.G. Spalding & Bros, the spaldeen was a pale pink, hollow rubber ball – about the size and feel of a freshly shaven tennis ball – which was indispensable to a multiplicity of popular urban street games. Girls used spaldeens in playing jacks, and for a number of rhythmic bouncing-rhyming games similar to those involving skipping ropes. Boys played games such as stoopball and stickball, which were variations on the rules and forms of baseball.

The word 'spaldeen' appears to be a Hibernicism, adding the Gaelic diminutive 'een' to the first syllable of the maker's name. Another theory is that the word may derive from *pillini*, Italian for a small ball, and corrupted in America to 'balleen', the name used for the target ball in *bocce*, the Italian version of bowls. As the word spaldeen is of an exclusively New York usage, it is perhaps fitting that its true etymology is lost in the mists of the melting pot.

Albert Goodwill Spalding, founder of the sporting goods firm, also set up in 1904 the Mills Commission the purpose of which was to prove that baseball was not derived from similar old English games – notably rounders – but had (with a boost from an obscure

TOP RIGHT Kids on the streets of Harlem playing the long-established NY game of stickball.

BOTTOM RIGHT Much of New York's sports culture starts with children's games on the street.

BELOW Italian New Yorkers playing the time-honoured game of *bocce* (or *bocci*), the Italian version of bowls or the French *boul*.

SPALDEEN

CENTRAL PARK

TOP Skiers in Central Park crossing the Bow Bridge in mid-winter.

ABOVE LEFT Softball in Central Park, always a site for amateur sports.

ABOVE RIGHT The Park also attracts roller skaters, cyclists and suchlike.

Army officer named Abner Doubleday)
sprung full grown, like Topsy, from the
natural genius of the American Boy. The
Doubleday myth was nonsense, but it is
ironic that Spalding's product was a vehicle
through which the ingenuity of New York's
children was exercised in devising games that
could be played within an extremely cramped
cityscape. Continuing civic improvements in
New York included the laying out of many
parks and playgrounds – notably Olmstead's
and Vaux's great Central Park in the middle
of Manhattan – but for most New York
youngsters, especially in the slums, the streets
remained the main place of recreation.

Stoopball derives its name from the stone
steps built on to the fronts of old New York
houses – from the Dutch word *stoep* – the ball
being put in play by ricocheting it off the
corner of the step. Its attractions as a game are
the elimination of the pitcher and an almost
infinite flexibility. Stickball, the great New
York street game, was also adaptable and the
rules could be varied and improvised to fit the
space available. Classic long street New York
stickball was simply baseball played with a
spaldeen and a broomhandle. The game was
usually played in narrow crosstown streets –
the wider north–south avenues having too
much traffic – the field being the floor of
a noisy canyon of brick or brownstone
tenement buildings. In its heyday New York
stickball produced some extraordinarily
skilled players and some – as with
present-day playground basketball players –
had reputations that went beyond the
folklore of the streets. The baseball great,
Willie Mays played in the streets of Harlem
during his days with the New York Giants.
He was a good stickball player but not by
any means the best.

The spaldeen is no longer made, and
although similar balls are available and some
sports shops sell purpose-made stickball balls,
the game is not as prevalent now as it once
was. Few street games are. Basketball is
undoubtedly the most played game in the
City nowadays. Economy of space means that
there is scarcely a public park or playground
in New York that doesn't have hoops. Any
number can play. There is a court at Third
Street and Sixth Avenue where, weather
permitting, the pick-up games have usually
begun by 10 a.m. and continue until dark.

BELOW The hot summers
in New York have always
provided an excuse for
improvised water sports
with neighbourhood kids.

Many talented players come from all over the City to play at Third Street. Among them are a number who, for one reason or another (often drugs), have slipped out of the organised (and supervised) sports programmes found in New York's schools, clubs and other youth organisations: those places where the sports-minded kid moves from the creative anarchy of the streets and develops into the trained athlete. Some of these, regardless of how objectively impossible their dreams have become, still aspire to play professionally.

THE TOUGHEST FANS IN THE WORLD

The followers of New York City's professional sports teams regard themselves – with some justice – the most ardent and knowledgeable in the country. Fierce in both commitment and criticism, nothing arouses their contempt more than the type of laid-back 'fan' found in say, Los Angeles, who arrives at the game during the third inning, gawps at the celebrities in the box seats for an hour and leaves before the end of the game no matter how tense the action.

Starting with the Mutuals club of the 1871 National Association there has been at least one New York and/or Brooklyn team in every major league since the inception of

ABOVE New York kids in one of the hundreds of inner-city basketball courts.

BELOW The now-legendary 'Goose' Tatum, the clown prince and star player with the Harlem Globetrotters.

RIGHT The most famous basketball side in the world, here at practice, the Harlem Globetrotters.

BASKE

TBALL

professional baseball. The same is true of pro football, the NY Rangers ice hockey team and basketball's New York Knicks who are founder members of their respective leagues.

The New York Yankees are the oldest continuing sports franchise in the City, and the most successful in the history of American professional sports. Imported from Baltimore in 1903 and initially called the Highlanders, the club had little success until 1920, when it bought Babe Ruth from the Boston Red Sox. Building on Ruth's enormous gifts and popularity (Yankee Stadium, erected in 1923, was called 'The House That Ruth Built'), between 1921 and 1964 the Yankees won 29 American League pennants and 20 World Series champion-ships. Success over the following decades was more erratic, the Yankee's World Series title in 1996 being their first since 1978. The team is one that has traditionally generated both passionate support and equally heartfelt loathing. Many have gloried in Yankee triumphs over the years, but the City also has many inveterate Yankee-haters. These have not only found the success monotonous but also felt the organisation to be arrogant, mean-spirited and racist. To root for the Yankees, a popular saying had it, was like rooting for US Steel.

BABE RUTH

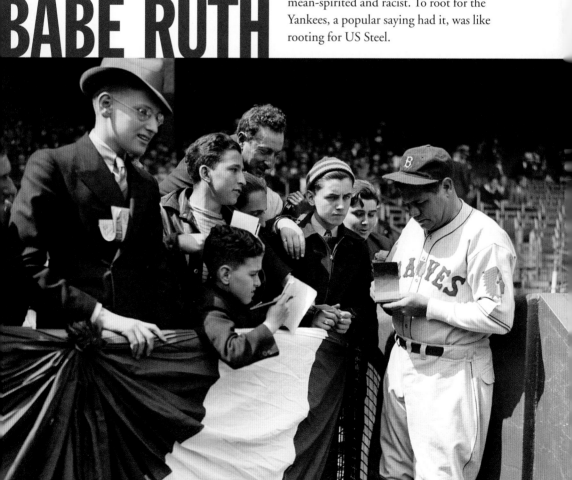

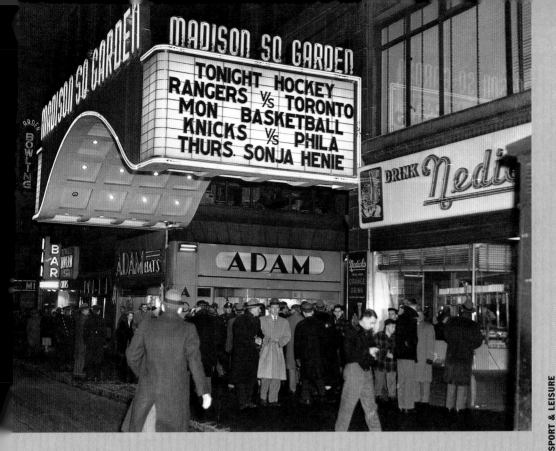

The most virulent Yankee-haters were, of course the fans of the New York Giants and the Brooklyn Dodgers. Fierce as the rivalry was between these two National League clubs, their fans were united in their loathing of the Yankees.

The Giants have roots going back to the 19th century, and from 1910 played their games at the Polo Grounds on Eighth Avenue and 155th Street. Led by the pugnacious manager, John McGraw, and with stars such as pitcher, Christy Mathewson, the Giants were a dominant force in the National League during the first quarter of the 20th century. They also had pennant-winning teams in the mid-30s; and in the three years after World War II they vied for National League supremacy with the Dodgers in games that often resembled open warfare. The most famous of these was the third and deciding game of the 1951 National League play-off in which Bobby Thomson hit his 'shot heard around the world', the two-out bottom-of-the-ninth, three-run homer which won the game and the pennant for the Giants.

The Brooklyn club also has origins going back to the 19th century, and from 1912 played at Ebbets Field. It was perhaps the intimacy of the club's Flatbush ballpark that made Dodgers fans identify so closely with the team. For many years it would not have

ABOVE Madison Square Garden – an exterior shot in 1948 with billing for ice hockey, basketball and skating star Sonja Henie.

BELOW Three million Yankees fans greeted their team after their winning the 1996 World Series.

LEFT Babe Ruth, when he was playing for the Boston Braves, signing autographs at the New York Giants' Polo Grounds, 1935.

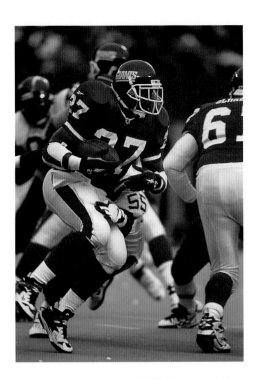

been the club's success: between the wars the Dodgers ('dem Bums') were a by-word for mediocrity. All that changed, however, with the coming of the 40s. Of the sixteen World Series played between 1941 and 1956, twelve featured at least one New York club and eight were 'Subway Series' with two local teams pitted against each other. This period is often regarded as the Golden Age of New York sports. As well as the City's baseball dominance, the football Giants, the Rangers and the Knicks were consistently competitive in their sports. For many, this era ended abruptly in 1957 when the Dodgers' owner, Walter O'Malley, moved the club to Los Angeles, after New York City refused to build him a new stadium. This was followed by the Giants' decision to follow the Dodgers west and relocate in San Francisco. The trauma caused by these moves is summed up in the story of two Brooklyn-reared newspaper men who decided over their beer one day that each would write down the names of the three most evil men of the century, and then compare lists. The first, a liberal, wrote: 'Adolph Hitler, Joseph Stalin and Walter O'Malley'. The other, more right wing wrote, 'Joseph Stalin, Adolph Hitler and Walter O'Malley'.

National League baseball returned to the City in 1962 in the form of the New York Mets. Despite being, in its early years,

ABOVE There are two New York Giants, the baseball team and the football side.

LEFT The huge crowds lining the streets for the Brooklyn Dodgers victory parade in 1941, when they won the National League pennant for the first time in 21 years.

BELOW Yankee Stadium: food vendors have a field day at major league games.

ODGERS

ABOVE Mets, Giants,
Dodgers and Yankees
supremo Casey Stengel
during his Yankees years.

RIGHT The New York Mets
at their home ground Shea
Stadium, Flushing, Queens.

INSET RIGHT The Mets'
star pitcher from the
1980s, Dwight Gooden.

perhaps the worst team in the history of
major league baseball the club endeared
itself to its New York fans who were
delirious when the 'Miracle Mets' of
1969 won the World Series.

An almost constant figure in New York
baseball for over 50 years was Casey Stengel:
'The Ol' Professor'. Stengel played for both
the Dodgers and Giants during his 1912–25
playing career. He managed the Dodgers
during their doldrum years and piloted the
Yankees through their most successful 50s
decade. He returned to become the Mets' first
manager, coined the term 'Amazin' for the
team, and famously asked 'Can't anybody
here play this game?'

Success is not a *sine qua non* for popularity
with New York sports fans. They can be
generous to the loser who has given his all.
Equally they can be ruthless towards an
athlete who is seen as not showing the game,
the team and the fans their due respect. Some
players have been hounded out of town by
such disapproval and by the relentless media
exposure that goes with playing in New York.

In 1985 the Mets' young pitcher Dwight
Gooden had a truly phenomenal season,
posting a won-lost record of 24-4 and leading
the league in every important pitching
statistic. The club was just squeezed out of
the National League East Championship by
the St Louis Cardinals who finished the
season three games up on the Mets. One
Mets fan – an archetypal old school New
York sporting man who was raised in the
shadow of the Polo Grounds and whose
ashes were scattered on the finishing line at
Belmont Park race track – commented: 'If
that bum Gooden don't drop those four
games we win the Division.'

GIANTS

METS

Text: Gary Vena

Chita Rivera and Ken LeRay in the original 1957 Broadway production of *West Side Story*. With music by Leonard Bernstein and lyrics by Stephen Sondheim, the Jerome Robbins' musical took Shakespeare's *Romeo and Juliet* and adapted it to the situation of rival gangs of whites and Puerto Ricans on New York's West Side.

THEATRE &

164-187
LITERATURE

Broadway, just for the record, is the name of the long New York street that extends from lower Manhattan near the Statue of Liberty to the Bronx, directly north. But the word is also synonymous with 'theatre', represented by a magical radius of city cross streets bustling with traffic and dotted with landmark playhouses whose illuminated signs signal the pulse and heartbeat of the 'Great White Way', a nostalgic reference from a bygone era.

The Broadway theatre district in New York is a happy state of mind: an oasis of live musicals, comedies and straight plays reinventing the world eight times a week, matinees included, and espousing *The New Yorker* critic Brendan Gill's credo that 'the first rule of life is to have a good time'. If the success of a typical theatre season is distinguished by the number of playhouses in use, or of tickets sold, or of Tony Awards bestowed on the hottest show in town, then Broadway remains a thriving enterprise in an ever-changing metropolis, forever flaunting its reputation as the 'fabulous invalid'.

Playgoers also caught up in the midtown frenzy tend to overlook several prestigious institutions located close by: two major opera companies, including the internationally renowned Metropolitan Opera; two dance companies long distinguished as the New York City Ballet and the American Ballet Theatre; a thriving New York Philharmonic; and two playhouses equipped with thrust stages – one larger, one more intimate – respectively named for their patrons, Vivian Beaumont and Mitzi Newhouse. So serious was it the dream of performance artists and city planners to develop a second oasis for the lively arts, that, by the late 1960s, each of the aforementioned occupied a permanent home at the Lincoln Centre, just north of the theatre district.

This successful venture expanded a landscape cultivated more than 200 years earlier when the British took over the original Dutch colony and built playhouses to showcase repertory favourites. The colonials were hooked. Merchant class audiences with the pretensions of a bourgeois aristocracy took a particular fancy to the colourful London imports, enlisting New York as fertile territory for further artistic talent between Broadway and London's West End.

Local playwrights established their own literary voice once the colonies won their independence from Britain, forging drama in which the characters and dialogue were indelibly American. When Royall Tyler's comedy, *The Contrast*, opened at the John Street Theatre in lower Manhattan on 16 April 1787, both the city and the American company which staged the work shook hands over its dazzling reception. The play's commercial viability led to subsequent

LEFT Broadway – 'The Great White Way' – has long come to represent neon lights, nightlife and, most of all, the theatre.

BELOW Henry James (1843–1916), New York-born writer, whose novels included *The Europeans* and *The Wings of the Dove*.

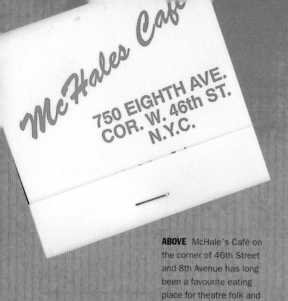

ABOVE McHale's Café on the corner of 46th Street and 8th Avenue has long been a favourite eating place for theatre folk and their audiences alike.

performances in other eastern cities and established a tradition in which the success of a New York première often determined what the rest of America could expect to see in their own local playhouses. For better or for worse, Broadway continues to be the arbiter of the country's taste in entertainment.

Amid rapid urban expansion and industrialisation during the latter half of the 19th century, the New York stage welcomed an important theatrical style – and the latest foreign import – which effectively mirrored the turbulent experiences of growing up in America. Melodrama, as it was popularly called, nourished the eclectic, often vulgar tastes of playgoers who eagerly identified with its colourful stereotypes, especially the innocent heroes and heroines. Cheering the underdog or hissing the villain came easily to the inhabitants of an uncompromising city, where good or bad luck determined one's economic success or financial ruin.

The thrill of special effects – such as the hero who found himself tied to a railway track in the face of an oncoming train – extended the dream and fantasy of audiences who imagined themselves on stage. The city, eerily personified, became an adversary in melodramas like Augustin Daly's *Under The Gaslight* and Edward Sheldon's *Salvation Nell*, whose heroine wistfully sighs, 'If everyone only let Christ do what he pleased with 'em, we'd have heaven right here in New York.' The messages were also uplifting, as the *ingénue* in Clyde Fitch's *The City* exclaims: 'Who wants to smell new-mown hay if he can breath in the gasoline on Fifth Avenue instead! Think of the theatres! The crowds! Think of being able to go out on the street and see someone you didn't even know by sight!'

By the turn of the century, the heart of the theatrical district had gravitated north. Times Square, nearly 30 years in the making, was transformed into the largest and most concentrated entertainment centre in the city's – and nation's – history, spelling big business and celebrity for savvy entrepreneurs and talented show people, respectively.

EUGENE O'NEILL

The conventions of melodrama were still tied to the past, however. The legitimate drama was ripe for innovation, which eventually

NORMAN MAILER

BELOW Writer and critic Norman Mailer was born in New Jersey in 1923 and grew up in Brooklyn. In 1948 he achieved fame with his novel *The Naked and the Dead*, which offered a harsh view of war and the nature of American society. Most subsequent work also involved social criticism of one kind or another. In 1979 he won the Pulitzer Prize for *The Executioner's Song*.

came from the brooding imagination of a young playwright working at the Princetown Playhouse in Greenwich Village, New York's Bohemia before World War I. His name was Eugene O'Neill.

Angry with his father, the 19th-century American actor James O'Neill, for wasting a brilliant acting career in the title role of *The Count Of Monte Cristo*, a popular melodrama that preserved his reputation while earning easy fortunes, Eugene O'Neill chose play-writing as his outlet to revolt against the theatrical artifice represented by his father's world. Audiences flocked to *The Emperor Jones*, which premièred at the Provincetown on 1 November 1920. But the success of *Beyond The Horizon* and *Anna Christie*, two full-length works which opened on Broadway the following season, proved a turning point in his career and set the American drama in a bold new direction. Impressively characterised by an unadorned realism that heralded something daring and new for uptown audiences, both plays won critical accolades, including Pulitzer Prizes.

Under the auspices of the prestigious Theatre Guild, a one-of-a-kind organisation that gave the playwright solid audience support through its recently instituted subscription policy, O'Neill's subsequent plays after 1928 were given first-rate productions. He was also in excellent company, sharing the spotlight with international favourites like Bernard Shaw and Luigi Pirandello. So universal in scope was the impact of his dramatic art by the 1930s that he received the Nobel Prize for Literature in 1936, bringing further distinction to the same Broadway establishment that now acclaimed other playwrights of his generation, including Elmer Rice, Maxwell Anderson, Sidney Howard, Philip Barry, Clifford Odets, William Saroyan and Thornton Wilder. Ironically, some of his finest work, including *A Touch Of The Poet*, *A Moon For Misbegotten* and *Long Day's Journey Into the Night*, had yet to be written. Their confessional tone would spark critical controversy in posthumous Broadway productions, profoundly influencing the playwrights who followed.

CHUMLEY'S

1928-1988

60TH ANNIVERSARY

ABOVE Chumley's, the ex-speakeasy on Bedford Street, Greenwich Village, has been frequented by most of New York's literati including O'Neill, John Steinbeck, Jack Kerouac, Lillian Hellman and many, many more.

LEFT The Times Square area on Broadway.

BELOW Eugene O'Neill (1888–1953) in 1933.

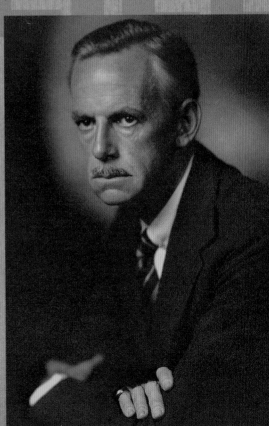

TENNESSEE WILLIAMS

'He gave birth to the modern American drama and died for it,' wrote Tennessee Williams, recalling his own personal struggle to succeed on Broadway a generation later. Williams was at home with the well-made play format, which not only appealed to Broadway tastes, but also accommodated his unusual blend of realism and poetic language. The results, best described as poetic realism, merged the elements he had absorbed from American stage realism and expressionism as well as European symbolism. The style was eloquently demonstrated in his first play, *The Glass Menagerie*, which proved quite popular with audiences when it opened on 31 March 1945. During the next ten years, he would establish himself as the most important American playwright to appear since O'Neill, standing tall among playwright contemporaries like Arthur Miller, William Inge, Robert Anderson and Edward Albee.

Unlike O'Neill, Williams' dialogue illuminated the embattled world of his characters, while his bold themes explored the American dream which had quietly disintegrated under the pressure of materialist expectations and had come to haunt so many artists of his contemporary post-war generation. Intending to shock conventional Broadway standards, his obsession with the seamy side of human behaviour, enhanced by eccentric but often luminous stage characters, infused plays that proved commercially viable in New York, across America, and abroad.

The most famous of these was *A Streetcar Named Desire*, which achieved its legendary status shortly after opening at the Barrymore Theatre on 3 December 1947 under the direction of Ekia Kazan. If audiences the world over have been unanimous in their approval of the play, which introduced the doomed Blanche DuBois to Williams' circle of unforgettable stage characters, certainly Marlon Brando's explosive and emotionally raw performance as Stanley Kowalski was no less memorable for establishing the method actor 'prototype' that served as the model for the generation of actors around him.

Unbeknown to most playgoers privileged to witness Brando on stage, the inspiration for his realistic portrayal, preserved in the 1951 film version, could be traced back to the first visit made by the Moscow Art Theatre to

ABOVE Tennessee Williams, photographed just after the 1945 opening on Broadway of his debut play, *The Glass Menagerie*.

LEFT From the 1947 production of *A Streetcar Named Desire*, with (left to right) Jessica Tandy, Rudy Bond and a young Marlon Brando.

BELOW Greenwich Village was a centre for the 'Beat Generation' writers of 50s America. Here the most celebrated of them all, Jack Kerouac, voices his contribution to a 'collective' poem being composed in a bookstore on West 14th Street in December, 1959.

New York nearly 25 years earlier, when several actors chose to remain behind and teach Stanislavski's controversial 'system'.

THE METHOD AND AFTER

The work of these actors had a profound effect on the lives of Stella Adler and Lee Strasberg, who became the foremost interpreters of Stanislavski's art and would exact their own influence on the impressionable Brando years later. Broadway, as well as movies, were never quite the same.

The other Williams play that proved momentous was *Summer and Smoke*, which failed on Broadway the season after *Streetcar* opened and was revived four years later by a fledgling theatre company working in the cramped quarters of a Greenwich Village theatre named for its unusual design, the Circle-In-The-Square. News of the production caught the attention of Brooks Atkinson, drama critic for the *New York Times*, who wrote an exceedingly favourable review that salvaged the play's reputation and brought acclaim to an unknown actress named Geraldine Page. Even more important, Atkinson formally acknowledged the existence of a legitimate theatre district outside the midtown area. Thus 'Off-Broadway' was born.

The occasion was auspicious and timely. On one hand, the American theatre, by mid-century, could no longer ignore the artistic upheaval and revolutionary changes that were sweeping through the theatres of Europe. On the other, the dynamics of producing mainstream theatre on Broadway were shifting under increased artistic and financial pressures. The impact resounded in New York, validating Off-Broadway's mission to offer less conservative or non-mainstream forms of theatre at affordable prices. Audiences eager to support the adventurous enterprise, which ushered in the plays of Samuel Beckett, Harold Pinter, Edward Albee, Jean Genet, Arthur Kopit and LeRoi Jones among many others, promptly filled the intimate playhouses situated on the outskirts of the commercial theatre district, like the Cherry Lane, the Sheridan Square Playhouse, the Phoenix Theatre and the Circle-In-The-Square. The press provided invaluable coverage that ultimately assisted in their growth and popularity.

ABOVE Filmmaker and actor Woody Allen has made his native New York the setting of most of his films – including 1979's *Manhattan*, in which black-and-white photography provided a perfect evocation of the city.

ABOVE LEFT A magazine stand in Greenwich Village. New York's bookstores and magazine stands offer the greatest reading choice anywhere on earth.

LEFT Playwright LeRoi Jones on the occasion of his play *The Toilet* opening Off-Broadway in 1964.

OFF-OFF-BROADWAY

Broadway suddenly faced healthy competition from artists willing to work without the financial backing needed uptown. As a result, productions abounded throughout the 1960s, welcoming both new works and old into intimate Off-Broadway surroundings. But the theatrical landscape was about to be upstaged once more as Off-Broadway enterprises gradually grew less adventurous. The call for totally uninhibited forms of theatrical expression needed to make room for an altogether different vanguard which, like its predecessor, would be named for where it pitched tent – Off-Off-Broadway.

Embracing ventures unsuitable for Off-Broadway and uptown audiences, theatre practitioners perfectly willing to test their wings in loft spaces, church basements, cafés and the backrooms of bars, joined the feisty new movement. Many of them failed. But others, like the Café Cino, Café La Mama, Judson Pet's Theatre, Performance Group, American Place Theatre and the Open Theatre, demonstrated a lasting style and influence, even if some of them could not keep their doors open forever.

Fuel for this often radical OOB movement was supplied by the cultural revolution that had shaken America. Issues relating to civil rights, gender equality, employment *vs* welfare, societal drop-outs, the drug culture and the emergence of rock music with its violent undercurrents were abetted by a postmodern paranoia that had quietly reared its head during America's lengthy involvement in Vietnam. Using viable theatre alternatives as a way to confront social and political concerns, these artists expanded the quantity and quality of performances to a level the city had not beheld in decades, when 50 or 60 new straight plays would open on Broadway each season.

Once the postmodern temperament had permeated American culture by the mid-1970s, however, Broadway seemed more receptive to the darker moods generated in the work of younger playwrights. Producers were understandably wary of mismatching the theatrical product with its target audience, although they also surmised that the lines of demarcation had grown blurry.

Like Pinter and Albee before him, David Mamet won the approval of Off-Broadway

ABOVE The Café La Mama, at 66 East 4th Street in the East Village, 1965.

BELOW Ellen Stewart, the director of La Mama, the theatre group of which went on to tour worldwide.

CAFE CINO

ABOVE Café Cino, the
theatre café founded by
Joe Cino in the 1960s,
located in Cornelia Street
in the West Village.

LA MAMA

KINGKONG

ABOVE One of the enduring images in New York-based fiction was that from the movie *King Kong*, when the giant ape scales the Empire State Building.

LEFT Playwright Neil Simon stands outside the Neil Simon Theatre, 1983.

RIGHT Barrymores is a popular restaurant and bar in the centre of New York's theatreland, named after the famous American theatrical dynasty.

BARRYMORES RESTAURANT
267 WEST 45th ST. 391-8400

WHITNEY SYSTEMS INC.

audiences before making a significant move uptown in 1975, where the popularity of *American Buffalo*, followed by the success of *Glengarry Ross* and *Speed The Plow*, demonstrated his remarkable crossover appeal. Mamet could be a sellout on Broadway, despite his unconventional style and fascination for eccentric characters who chronicled the unethical games that people play. Still, his success could not explain the elusive, often deceptive conditions of New York's theatrical landscape, and one that offered no safe guarantees for fellow playwright Sam Shepherd.

Nurtured by the alternative theatre movement of the 1960s, Shepherd explored the schizophrenic ethos of his own generation in theatrical styles that were boldly realised in many prestigious Off-Broadway playhouses. That his plays never crossed over to the other side, or needed to for that matter, was further proof of the growing non-mainstream venue where artists of his calibre could meet audiences on their own special terms.

Like a coin whose unmatched halves reflect whole but separate images, both the mainstream and non-mainstream illuminate vastly different landscapes of the dramatic art they serve: from the poetic realism of Tina Howe, Lanford Wilson and Jon Robin Baitz, to the thematic variations on the popular comedy-of-manners style in A.R. Gurney, Wendy Wasserstein, Alfred Uhry and John Guare. A lopsided universe informs the dramatic imaginations of David Margulies, Richard Greenburg, Paula Vogel and John Patrick Shanley, yielding bittersweet repercussions. The isolation of 'otherness' imbues the work of David Henry Hwang, Terrence McNally and Marsha Norman. There are the politics of anger in Tony Kushner and the politics of disenfranchisement in August Wilson. There is, too, the perennial nostalgia of Neil Simon, representing Broadway's enduring comic tradition.

From the Lincoln Centre to Broadway, from Off-Broadway to the lower eastside, the theatrical scene has always cherished a split personality of its own making, never needing to assert one persona over the other. The happier and brighter mask, no less important than its serious one, has adorned an exciting tradition of musical theatre since the close of the 19th century when variety acts drew wild

ABOVE David Mamet before the opening of *American Buffalo* at St Clements Church in January 1976.

BELOW The other side of Broadway theatre was based in Vaudeville – this playbill dates from 1897.

PARK THEATRE

WM. BARRY, - - - - - - - - - Manager
JACK C. HUFFMAN, - - - - - - - Director

Week commencing Monday Matinee, Sept. 13, 1897
MATINEE EVERY DAY.

AN OLIO OF HIGH-GRADE VAUDEVILLE.

The Latest European Novelty,
Walter—*THE GREAT DEAVES*—Mamie
And their Laughable Troupe of Merry Manikins.
See the Funny Clown, Midway Dancer, Gymnasts, Acrobats, Singers, Dancers.
Wait for the Bull.

The Real Hebrew Character,
JOE WELCH
Originator of this style of entertainment.

LILLIE WESTERN
The Vaudeville's Premier Musical Artiste

LOTTERY OF LOVE,

An Eccentric Comedy, in Three Acts, by and produced by special arrangement
with AUGUSTIN DALY.

Under the direction of JACK C. HUFFMAN.
CAST OF CHARACTERS.

Adolphus Doubledot	Howell Hansel
Benjamin Buttercorn	William Barry
Capt. Sam Merrimac	William Davidge
Tom Dangerous	Ernest Esmond
David	Walter Stuart
Rye	Samuel Forrest
Grass	R. Harold Davidge
Jo	Henrietta Crossman
Mrs. Zenobia Sherramy	Maggie Harold
Diana	Anna Layng
Ann Eliza	Daisy Lovering

ACT I.—Doubledot's residence, at Riverdale. Afternoon of first wedding.

ACT II.—Buttercorn's villa, Newport. Two years later. The afternoon of a second bridal.

ACT III.—Same as Act II. Two minutes' wait.

applause from audiences who packed the balconies of White Way. As Broadway's hottest baby, vaudeville was already the nation's most popular form of live entertainment, thanks to enterprising producers who knew how to package and promote this joyful commodity through elaborate circuits established across America.

Unlike burlesque, with its accent on low comedy and sex, vaudeville provided wholesome family entertainment whose appeal was rooted in the immigrant experience. Its ingredients struck warm chords with the melting pot mentality of New York audiences who were no doubt reminded of the music-hall entertainments of their native homelands.

VAUDEVILLE

Catering for a newly fashioned American sensibility, however, these talented singers, dancers, acrobats and comedians helped audiences discover how universal and infectious the sound of laughter could be. Audiences cheered Weber and Fields, Al Jolson and Jimmy Durante, and fell in love with the antics of a husband-and-wife team that called itself, quite simply, Burns and Allen – the same George and Gracie who brought their unique comic gifts to the movies and television after vaudeville's demise by the late 1920s.

For without much warning, the advent of 'talkies' revitalised the art of silent pictures overnight, ousting prized vaudevillians from the stage. Seeing the handwriting on the wall, many were smart enough to jump ship, unless they were among the lucky ones, like Fanny Brice, who was plucked from vaudeville and put into the Follies by Flo Ziegfeld himself. The likes of W.C. Fields and Sophie Tucker found stardom in Hollywood or at New York's more fashionable supperclubs which were now headlining sophisticated speciality acts. Other vaudevillians just crossed their fingers, hoping the nightmare would pass.

Left with even fewer options, burlesque dwindled into striptease, further outraging moralists who eventually won permission in 1942 to shut down the city's few remaining burlesque houses. Talkies, in the meantime, surpassed all expectations, giving movie moguls and rising starlets all the attention they could possibly crave at splashy Broadway

RIGHT A scene from the original 1927 Broadway production of *Show Boat*.

BELOW From 1935, the Ziegfeld Follies could be seen at the Winter Gardens Theatre, with a cast including Bob Hope and Fannie Brice.

RIGHT The burlesque and vaudeville team of Joseph Weber (left) and Lew Fields.

ABOVE From the 1950 stage production of *Guys and Dolls*, Robert Alda (father of actor Alan Alda) as Sky Masterson and Isabel Bigley as Sister Sarah Brown.

BELOW The fabulous burlesque queen Gypsy Rose Lee (1914–1970) in a publicity shot by Bruno of Hollywood and New York.

premières. The Broadway-to-Hollywood route became a viable option for a privileged circle of stage actors who enjoyed the challenge of live theatre and the celebrity status afforded by films.

Nourished by numerous remarkable transformations, from its origins in the minstrel show which laid the essential groundwork, to its classier connections with late 19th-century European operetta, the Broadway musical has remained indestructible since its inception. The formulaic period kept audiences smiling through the first 40 years of the 20th century – not a bad track record. It thrived on clichéd characters and comical situations which offered plenty of opportunity to showcase one musical number after another. There were notable exceptions of course, like Jerome Kern and Oscar Hammerstein II's *Show Boat*, produced in 1927, which was distinguished by its integration of book, music and choreography. It was a true American saga, surpassing the musicals of its own time as well as those still to be written. It spoke in a genuine American idiom, an innovation that helped immortalise Edna Ferber's wonderful characters, as revivals have repeatedly shown.

Yet *Show Boat* was not considered revolutionary. That distinction belonged to *Oklahoma!*, produced 16 years later, in which Rogers and Hammerstein's musical score, seamlessly interwoven with Agnes DeMille's

ABOVE The original St James Theatre (West 48th Street) playbill for the opening run of *Oklahoma!* in October 1944.

BELOW Sheet music published during the first Broadway runs of *South Pacific*, *The Pajama Game* and *Kismet*.

homespun choreography, found exciting new ways to reveal the sentimental farm characters of *Green Grow The Lilacs*, the Lynn Riggs play on which the musical was based. The boy-meets-girl story was exactly what the Broadway musical was all about and what audiences were looking for now that America was at war. The critics unanimously agreed that *Oklahoma!* was a turning point and their verdict was sacrosanct.

The collaborations of Rogers and Hammerstein have formed the bedrock of the 20th-century Broadway musical, the achievement of a genuinely poetic folk-opera in masterpieces like *Carousel*, *South Pacific*, *The King and I* and *The Sound of Music*.

Embroidering upon our dreams and fantasies and transporting us to magical worlds at the wave of a baton, the allure of New York in all of its gritty and glittering splendour has inspired *On The Town*, *Guys and Dolls*, *West Side Story* and *Rent*. The romance and intrigue of the Great White Way have been glorified in *Kiss Me Kate*, *Funny Girl*, *42nd Street* and *Follies*. Where else but on Broadway could the exploits of burlesque's most famous practitioner, Gypsy Rose Lee, inspire four top collaborators – Arthur Laurents, Jule Styne, Stephen Sondheim and Jerome Robbins – to create one helluva musical comedy which they called *Gypsy*? The novelty of *Damn Yankees*, the charm of *Sweet Charity*, the antics of

PLAYBILL
a weekly magazine for theatregoers

The Broadway Theatre

WEST SIDE STORY

ABOVE The Broadway
Theatre *Playbill* magazine
for *West Side Story*, 1957.

A Funny Thing Happened on the Way to the Forum, the sentiment of *The Most Happy Fella*, the bravura of *Hello Dolly!*, the enchantment of *Kismet*, the cynicism of *Pal Joey*, the decadence of *Cabaret*, the universality of *Fiddler On The Roof* are all happy musical reminders of what Broadway has always done best.

There have been other showstoppers along the way, two of which were nurtured in workshop settings under the artistic direction of Joseph Papp. As one of the founders of the New York Shakespeare Festival, Papp was an important contributor to the city's theatrical life, both for his genuine support of American stage artists and for his interest in British and European imports. Countless productions were simultaneously showcased over many successful seasons down at the Public Theatre on Lafayette Street. But nobody, including Papp himself, was prepared for the excitement about to explode on Broadway.

The more controversial of the two was *Hair*, concocted as an 'American tribal rock musical' when it opened up on 29 April 1968. Its anti-war theme and outspoken messages of love were compatible with America's escalating hippie culture, giving it unofficial licence to break the rules, especially when cast members decided to shed their clothes on stage. The heavily publicised stunt, teasingly prompted by the marijuana high that filled the auditorium, became an essential part of every performance.

Fuelled by an audacity seemingly ill-suited for Broadway, *Hair* thrived on the courage of its convictions, demonstrating a genuine innocence that won the respect of delighted playgoers who kept returning for more. But its strongest message – albeit a silent one – was displayed in the lobby of the Biltmore Theatre, where foot-high numbers scrawled in chalk kept a daily count of American casualties in Vietnam. A musical with clout and a political conscience, *Hair* achieved a run of 1,742 performances and introduced thousands of young people to Broadway.

The second phenomenon brought distinction to the 1975 Broadway season, displaying an altogether different temperament. The Vietnam War was over, but a mood of cynicism still prevailed. As conceived by director Michael Bennett, *A Chorus Line* was groundbreaking for finding

its life and pulse in the real-life stories of its original cast members who spoke, sang, and danced their experiences into contemporary and bittersweet allegory. The balance of forthright characters, the absolute simplicity of the staging, the uninhibited dramatic action and the memorable score by Marvin Hamlisch and Edward Kleban collectively reinforced the versatility and natural appeal of the Broadway musical tradition. Disturbed but uplifted by the show's survival-of-the-fittest premise, New Yorkers knew it could not get much better than this.

Instead it got bigger. While no single person or event could take responsibility for the series of transformations ahead it was obvious that *A Chorus Line*'s spare design was a glowing exception to the Broadway rule. A different kind of energy had already been set into motion by Bob Fosse, Gower Champion and Tommy Tune whose indelible choreography and direction had formed the

ABOVE Members of the cast of *A Chorus Line* performing for the last time on Broadway at the Shubert Theatre after their record-breaking run.

BELOW *A Chorus Line* producer Joseph Papp raises his hand in salute, with the cast and a neon commemorating the 6,137 performances which ended on 29 April 1990.

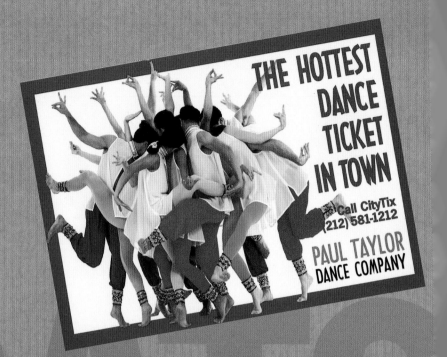

ABOVE Woody Allen surveys the Manhattan skyline on the set of *New York Stories*, 1989.

BELOW A montage of neon signs heralding the Lloyd Webber era of the musical, including *Cats*, *The Phantom of the Opera* and *Miss Saigon*.

underpinnings of the concept musical. Furthermore, Hal Prince's innovative stage direction had done as much for Sondheim's more artistic creations, elevating them to a stature that endured a lasting tradition.

Then something quite unexpected happened. An Englishman named Andrew Lloyd Webber came to town with a musical agenda that had little in common with Sondheim's. Taking the concept idea in a different direction, he seamlessly blended stage spectacle with sustained melodic lines to fashion a style that was unabashedly reminiscent of opera and often as adamant in its impact. Under the direction of Hal Prince, *Phantom of the Opera* opened at the Majestic Theatre on 26 January 1988, creating the kind of sensation that Broadway audiences had not experienced in years. Just around the corner at the Winter Garden was *Cats*, another Lloyd Webber success, which had first set up residence seven years earlier. Ready or not, the Broadway musical was caught in the throes of an exciting overhaul. Even more importantly, its inspiration had come from abroad.

It was evident by now that Broadway was becoming a two-way street. It used to be that a theatrical venture needed New York's stamp of approval for its passport to success. But in fact playgoers would be astonished at the number of commercial enterprises on Broadway and Off – both straight and musical – with the mark of non-profit regional theatre stamped on them somewhere. Or else they were imports.

Andrew Lloyd Webber did not achieve the reformation single-handedly. Help came from Alain Boublil and Claude-Michel Schonberg, whose collaborations – *Les Misérables* and *Miss Saigon* – coincided with this new agenda, providing healthy competition that nourished its popularity. Critics invented the word 'megahit' to describe the phenomenon.

Two of these landmark playhouses, the Lyric and the Apollo, have been merged into the new Ford Centre and become the home of a Canadian musical extravaganza imported to inaugurate the occasion. Inspired by E.L. Doctorow's novel, *Ragtime* is a hybrid in its depiction of ethnic groups and economic classes, a true microcosm of America's multicultural heritage, and a harbinger of an exciting new era for Broadway.

DIRECTORY

ARCHITECTURE

Brooklyn Bridge
South St/Dover St
(Manhattan side)

Chrysler Building
405 Lexington Avenue
(212) 682 3070

Citicorp Centre
153 East 53rd St
(212) 935 2200

Empire State Building
350 Fifth Avenue
(212) 736 3100

Flatiron Building
175 Fifth Avenue

**General Electric Building
(formerly RCA)**
570 Lexington Avenue

Grand Central Station
East 42nd St/Park Avenue
(212) 340 3000

India House
Hanover Square

Rockefeller Centre
47–50th Sts

St Patrick's Cathedral
457 Madison Avenue
(212) 935 3960

Seagram Building
375 Park Avenue
(212) 572 7000

Statue of Liberty
Liberty Island
(212) 363 3200

United States Courthouse
40 Centre St

US Custom House
1 Bowling Green St
(212) 668 6624

Waldorf Astoria
301 Park Avenue
(212) 355 3000

Woolworth Building
233 Broadway

World Financial Centre
West St
(212) 945 0505

World Trade Centre
Church St
(212) 435 4170

ART

MUSEUMS

Brooklyn Museum
200 Eastern Parkway
Brooklyn
(718) 638 5000

The Cloisters
Fort Tryon Park
(212) 923 3700

**Cooper-Hewitt Museum of
Decorative Arts and Design**
2 East 21st St
(212) 860 6868

Frick Collection
1 East 70th St
(212) 288 0700

Jewish Museum
1109 Fifth Avenue
(212) 423 3200

Metropolitan Museum of Art
1000 Fifth Avenue
(212) 535 7710

**Museum of Modern Art
(MoMA)**
11 West 53rd St
(212) 708 9400

**Museum of the City of
New York**
Fifth Avenue/103rd St
(212) 534 1672

National Academy of Design
1083 Fifth Avenue
(212) 369 4880

**Solomon R. Guggenheim
Museum**
1071 Fifth Avenue/88th St
(212) 423 3500

**Whitney Museum of
American Art**
945 Madison Avenue
(212) 570 3600

GALLERIES

Gagosian Gallery
980 Madison Avenue
(212) 744 2313

John Weber Gallery
142 Greene St
(212) 966 6115

Knoedler & Company
19 East 70th St
(212) 794 0550

Leo Castelli
420 West Broadway
(212) 431 5160

Mary Boone Gallery
417 West Broadway
(212) 752 2929

Pace Gallery
32 East 57th St
(212) 421 3292

Sidney Janis Gallery
110 West 57th St
(212) 586 0110

FESTIVALS

**Macy's Thanksgiving
Day Parade**
4th Thursday in November
Natural History Museum at
Central Park West to Macy's
at Herald Square

**Christmas Tree Lighting
Ceremony**
Early December
Rockefeller Centre

Hanukkah Menorah
Mid-December
Grand Army Plaza
Brooklyn

New Year's Eve:
Midnight Run starting
at Tavern on the Green,
Central Park;
Poetry readings in
St Mark's Church,
Second Avenue;
Fireworks in Central Park;
Times Square celebrations

Chinese New Year
Mid-January
Chinatown, around Mort St,
spilling into Little Italy and
Lower East Side

**Empire State Building
Run-Up**
Early February
Races to 102nd floor
of building

St Patrick's Day Parade
17 March
Fifth Avenue from 44th
to 86th Sts

**Greek Independence
Day Parade**
25 March
Fifth Avenue from 49th
to 59th Sts

Easter Flower Show
Week before Easter Sunday
Macy's Department Store
151 West 34th St
(212) 695 4400

Easter Parade
Easter Sunday
Fifth Avenue from 44th
to 59th Sts

Cherry Blossom Festival
Late April/early May
Brooklyn Botanic Garden

**Martin Luther King Jr
Day Parade**
Third Sunday in May
Fifth Avenue from 44th
to 86th Sts

Food Festival
Late May
Ninth Avenue from 37th
to West 57th Sts

Puerto Rico Day Parade
First Sunday in June
Fifth Avenue from 44th
to 86th Sts

Museum Mile Festival
Second Tuesday in June
Fifth Avenue from 82nd to
105th Sts

**Lesbian and Gay Pride
Day Parade**
Late June
Fifth Avenue from Columbus
Circle to Washington Square

**Independence Day
Fireworks Display**
4 July
East River waterfront

Out-of-Doors Festival
Summer and early autumn
Lincoln Centre

Shakespeare in the Park
June to September
Delacorte Theatre
Central Park

Von Streuben Day Parade
Third week in September
Upper Fifth Avenue

Feast of St Gennaro
Third week in September
Little Italy, with parade up
and down Mulberry St

Pulaski Day Parade
Sunday closest to 5 October
Fifth Avenue 26th to
52nd Sts

Columbus Day Parade
Second Monday in October
Fifth Avenue 44th to
86th Sts

Halloween Parade
31 October
Greenwich Village

New York Marathon
Last Sunday in October or
first Sunday in November
From Staten Island and
through all the city's
boroughs

FOOD & DRINK

RESTAURANTS & CAFÉS

Café des Artistes
1 West 67th St
(212) 877 3500

The Four Seasons
99 East 52nd St
(212) 754 9494

Golden Unicorn
18 East Broadway
(212) 941 0911

Gotham Bar & Grill
12 East 12th St
(212) 620 4020

Grand Central Oyster Bar
Grand Central Station
East 42nd St/Park Avenue
(212) 490 6650

Le Cirque
455 Madison Avenue
(212) 794 9292

Peter Luger Steakhouse
178 Broadway
Brooklyn
(718) 387 7400

The Rainbow Room
65th floor
General Electric Building
30 Rockefeller Plaza
(212) 632 5000

Sylvia's
328 Lenox Avenue
(212) 996 0660

TriBeCa Grill
375 Greenwich St
(212) 941 3900

Union Square Café
21 East 16th St
(212) 243 4020

Windows on the World
107th floor
World Trade Centre
West St
(212) 938 1111

BARS, DINERS & DELIS

Balducci's
424 Avenue of the Americas
(212) 673 2600

Bar Six
502 Sixth Avenue

Bowery Bar
40 East 4th St

The Cedar Tavern
University Place

Dean & DeLuca
560 Broadway
(212) 431 1691

The Ear Inn
326 Spring St

Empire Diner
Tenth Avenue/22nd St
Chelsea

Katz's Deli
205 East Houston St

McSorley's Old Alehouse
15 East 7th St

Nathan's Famous
Near boardwalk at corner
of Surf Avenue
Coney Island

Peculier Pub
145 Bleecker St

Tavern on the Green
Central Park
West 64th St

Zabar's
2245 Broadway
(212) 787 2000

MUSIC

VENUES

Apollo Theatre
253 West 125th St
(212) 749 5838

Beacon Theatre
2124 Broadway
(212) 496 7070

Carnegie Hall
881 Seventh Avenue
(212) 247 7800

Cotton Club
666 West 125th St
(212) 749 5838

Lincoln Centre
155 West 65th St
(212) 875 5400

Madison Square Garden
4 Pennsylvania Plaza
(212) 465 6741

Radio City Music Hall
50th St/Avenue of the
Americas
(212) 247 4777

Roseland
239 West 52nd St
(212) 247 0200

Showman's Café
2321 Eighth Avenue/
125th St

Village Vanguard
178 Seventh Avenue South
(212) 255 4037

CLUBS

Bitter End
147 Bleecker St
(212) 673 7030

Bottom Line
15 West 4th St
(212) 228 6300

CBGB
315 Bowery
(212) 982 4052

Knitting Factory
47 East Houston St
(212) 219 3055

Max's Kansas City
West 52nd St

Mercury Lounge
217 East Houston St
(212) 260 4700

S.O.B.'s
204 Varick St
(212) 243 4940

Tramps
45 West 21st St
(212) 727 7788

SPORT & LEISURE

AMERICAN FOOTBALL

Giants Stadium
Meadowlands
East Rutherford
New Jersey
(201) 935 8222 (Giants)
(201) 935 8500 (Jets)

BASEBALL

Yankee Stadium
River Avenue/161st St
The Bronx
(718) 293 6000

Shea Stadium
126th St/Roosevelt Avenue
Flushing
Queens
(718) 507 8499

BASKETBALL, BOXING & ICE HOCKEY

Madison Square Garden
Seventh Avenue/33rd St
(212) 465 MSG1

FITNESS CENTRES

YMCA 47th St
224 East 47th St
(212) 756 9600

YMCA West Side
5 West 63rd St
(212) 787 4400

HORSE RACING

Aqueduct Race Track
Ozone Park
Queens
(718) 641 4700

Belmont Park Race Track
Hempstead Turnpike
Long Island
(718) 641 4700

ICE SKATING

Plaza Rink
1 Rockefeller Plaza
Fifth Avenue
(212) 332 7654

Wollman Rink
Central Park
Fifth Avenue/59th St
(212) 396 1010

THEATRE

Barrymore Theatre
243 West 47th St
(212) 239 6200

Circle-in-the-Square
159 Bleecker St
(212) 254 6330

Delacorte Open-air Theatre
Central Park/81st St
(212) 861 7277

La MaMa
74A East 4th St
(212) 475 7710

Lincoln Centre
155 West 65th St
(212) 875 5400

Lyceum Theatre
149 West 45th St
(212) 239 6200

Majestic Theatre
245 West 44th St
(212) 239 6200

Provincetown Playhouse
133 MacDougal St
(212) 777 2571

Public Theatre
425 Lafayette St
(212) 539 8500

Sullivan Street Playhouse
181 Sullivan St
(212) 674 3838

Symphony Space
2537 Broadway
(212) 864 5400

Winter Garden
1634 Broadway
(212) 239 6200

PICTURE CREDITS